AF445314

WRITE YOUR NOVEL NOW!

100 TIPS & STRATEGIES TO HELP YOU DRAFT, REVISE, AND PUBLISH YOUR BOOK

BRIAN D. ROWE

First Paperback Edition: April 2020

For more information on Brian Rowe, please visit:
http://brianrowebooks.com

Write Your Novel Now! 100 Tips and Strategies to Help You Draft, Revise, and Publish Your Book
ISBN: 9798638847531

TABLE OF CONTENTS

INTRODUCTION

Welcome! Are you ready to write your novel now and not later?

I'm so excited to share with you 100 essays filled with awesome tips, tricks, and strategies that will help you in the planning, writing, revising, and publishing of your novel.

I should know what it takes to write a novel—I've written twenty of them in ten years. I write mostly young adult fiction, but I've also attempted middle grade and adult fiction throughout the years. I've written horror, thriller, romance, fantasy, contemporary, LGBTQ. I've tried all sorts of different things.

And one thing I've been serious about since the beginning is the necessity to finish what you start. The ability to write book after book with confidence.

I was so terrified to write my first novel ten years ago. I wasn't sure if I could do it. I wasn't sure if I'd make it past chapter one.

Here's the deal—writing the first draft of a novel isn't as scary as it looks. And in this book I'll share with you many important ways to give you the courage to finally write that novel!

I have split up the book into five sections—**Getting Started, Drafting & Storytelling, Revising & Editing, Publishing & Community,** and **Finally.** Feel free to read these essays from beginning to end, or by section if you'd like. It's entirely up to you!

So here we go. 100 tips and strategies to write, revise, and publish your novel. Are you ready to get started?

GETTING STARTED

1. 5 Ways to Develop a Killer Work Ethic as a Novel Writer

So you want to write more and not less?

Don't we all. We wake up every morning ready to write more, *wanting* to write more, but so often life gets in the way… and you get to bed that night not having written much at all.

Trust me, I've been there.

Many people have asked me over the years how I've managed to write twenty novels in ten years, how I manage to draft one novel after another and produce so damn much. Many think I have all day to work on my writing, when such is definitely not the case.

The thing is, no matter your schedule, you absolutely have the ability to create a better work ethic when it comes to your writing. In fact, you can develop a killer work ethic if you try!

Here are *five things* I do often that might help you in your writing journey…

1. Develop a writing schedule and stick to it.

I'll say it a hundred times in this book if I need to: *this* is the key to success as a writer. It's *figuring out a schedule* for when you're going to write and how much you're going to write and *sticking to that schedule* every single day until your project is finished.

As soon as you deviate from the schedule, you might deviate more in the days to come, and you might stop writing completely because you've given yourself permission to step away from your rigid schedule.

Here's the thing about developing a writing schedule: you need to figure one out that works best for you.

When I write my novels, I typically write 2,000 words a day every day until the first draft is done. This number is intimidating for some, so starting at 1,000 words a day or 500 words or even 200 words a day might work better for you.

Your writing schedule is totally up to you, and of course feel free to push yourself harder if your current schedule is working well or pull back a little if you can't find yourself reaching the minimum word count.

Whatever you do, stick to your schedule every day, and you will absolutely find yourself writing more.

2. Create deadlines for yourself.

Going beyond the writing schedule, you need to come up with *deadlines* to make your work ethic truly take off in ways you didn't think it could.

This is especially helpful for longer writing projects. It's not enough to simply create your daily writing schedule. You need to look far off in the future to see what possible date you might be able to reach THE END.

For example, this past summer I wrote the first draft of my twentieth novel. I started it on June 3, 2019, and I decided that day I would finish the novel on July 3, 2019.

One month to write the book, and to do that, I needed to write more than 2,000 words a day. So I actually aimed for 2,500 words a day at first, and then by week three, I was nearing or even going over 3,000 words a day. One day I even reached 4,000 words!

On July 3, I wrote the epilogue chapter and reached THE END, on the exact day I was hoping to finish the manuscript. The first draft came in at 81,000 words, about 5,000 words longer than I had hoped it'd be.

I was able to do this by coming up with a writing schedule, sticking to it, and keeping my firm deadline in mind always.

3. Plan your writing a day or even a week ahead.

This is kind of similar to developing a writing schedule and creating deadlines for yourself, but going a step further, what helps me maintain my killer work ethic is figuring out always not just what I'm writing today but also what I'm writing *tomorrow*, and even the next week or month.

Last summer I figured out exactly what I wanted to work on in my fiction for the rest of 2019. That's right—way back in August 2019 I figured out my writing projects, to the week, all the way through December 2019.

And I've done the same with most of 2020, too.

I always feel more confident about my work ethic when I know what's coming up. When I know what I'm working on tomorrow and next week. It actually gets me more excited when I have a clear idea of what's on my writing plate next.

The absolute worst thing you can do for your work ethic is sit down at your desk in the morning without a clue what you want to work on. You'll sit there, and you'll sit there, and nothing will get done!

So plan ahead. Figure out what your next project is days, weeks, even months in advance.

4. Do everything you can to avoid procrastination and erase all distractions.

Another easy way to ruin your work ethic is to procrastinate. Is to focus on something *else* for five minutes or ten minutes or an hour or whatever that don't do anything to help you reach your goal.

In 2020 we have so many distractions. There is just so much demanding your attention. Articles to read. Videos to watch. New television series to stream. The amount of content available to us now is insane.

You want to find pockets of your day to catch up on some of this content, of course. Don't try to avoid it all completely, you'll never be able to!

But what you need to do is push aside the distractions and procrastination during that sacred writing time *by any means possible*. For me, it's turning off the Wi-Fi right before I begin my fiction writing. Or putting on some music that inspires me. Or signing out of all my social media sites before I begin.

You might think a five-minute break to watch a Youtube video isn't much of a distraction, it's just something to help you relax. But you know what happens after that? You click on a second video, and a third. Before you know it, a whole hour is gone, an hour you could have spent writing!

You won't be able to avoid distractions all throughout the day, but if you have one hour, maybe two hours, to do your writing for the day, do everything you can to eliminate the distractions during that time so your work ethic can thrive.

5. Find your inspiration in other writers and creators.

Now this is a distraction you should embrace, not eliminate. Because reading the work of others that inspire you will actually do more for your work ethic than you know.

I write for at least two hours every day, seven days a week. I've been doing this for about a decade now. Some days this is easy for me to do. And other days it's a whole lot harder.

What always helps keep me motivated through the hard times is finding inspiration in other writers and creators. It's seeing the beautiful, harrowing work of others and wanting to push myself to do work just as good as them.

This is why I keep on average two to three books beside my bed. Nothing truly inspires me more to get my writing day started than twenty to thirty minutes of reading as soon as I wake up in the morning. I cherish this time of silence, this time of no screens.

I lose myself in a world for a short bit of time, and that process invites newfound creativity, newfound inspiration. It makes me want to do even better work in my writing hours to come.

Don't waste time scrolling through social media when you first wake up. Spend more time finding writing that inspires you to write something amazing for the day. To do something that you can be proud of.

For me, reading a chapter or two of a really good book will do this always. But it might be something different for you.

Just don't ignore the amazing writers and creators out there. Focusing on the work of others instead of the work of only yourself will actually help your work ethic improve in the weeks to come, I'm telling you!

Developing a killer work ethic won't happen overnight. Just keep at it, and you will get there.

It took me awhile to really find my rhythm, find my groove. I struggled writing my novels in the beginning. In my twenties I was distracted so easily and days and weeks would go by with little writing from me to be seen.

But things got better. Especially when I knew I could start a long writing project… and eventually finish it.

And as the years went by I developed more and more strategies to help me get more writing done, to help find a work ethic that's not only outstanding, but *killer*.

You can find that killer work ethic inside of you, too. You just need to develop a writing schedule and stick to it, create deadlines for yourself, plan ahead, avoid distractions, and find inspiration wherever you can get it.

Again, don't beat yourself up if you don't reach the amount of words you wanted to write today, and don't panic if you manage to miss a deadline here and there.

The important thing is to keep trying and *keep going*. As long as you learn from your mistakes and never give up, eventually you will get there!

2. 10 Things You Should Know Before Becoming a Novelist

1. The first drafts of novels are always hard, no matter how many books you've written.

The first draft of my first ever book was really hard, but when I finished it, I felt like I had climbed Mount Everest. The following year I managed to write four different novels. The year after that? I wrote three more.

I've slowed down lately, but I'm still going strong. I think my writing gets better with each new project I take on, but you know what stays the same? The *difficulty*. Even though I have more tricks up my sleeve today than I did in 2010, writing a first draft is always difficult.

Don't worry, though. What also remains the same is that it's exhilarating each and every time, too.

2. Your first novel will probably not be the first of your novels that gets published.

I self-published my first few books, so actually, in my case, the first book I ever wrote was the first book I ever published.

But looking back, I wouldn't advise you to introduce yourself to the world with your very first novel. And if you go the traditional publishing route, you're probably going to need two or three books, maybe more, before you get the attention of a literary agent or publisher.

I'm one to know: it took me *sixteen* novels before a literary agent took a chance on me. That's right, sixteen. And of those sixteen novels, I queried eight of them. Over seven years, I had some close calls on a few of my earlier projects, but it wasn't until I wrote a middle grade adventure story that everything changed for me.

3. Revision needs to go beyond two or three drafts done all by yourself.

One thing I learned the hard way, especially in my first few years of writing, was not taking enough time to revise. I'd say my first eight or nine manuscripts I worked really hard on the first draft, then sort of just drifted through the second and third drafts, changing sentences, adding a little description here and there, but not really looking *critically* at the project as a whole.

Therefore, a lot of my early work suffered, especially when I moved into the querying process. After you finish the first draft of a novel, you really do want to send it out, trust me, I know. You want to move past the revising part and get an agent, get a publishing deal, get paid your million bucks.

But unfortunately, all that time you invested in writing the first draft becomes a total waste if you breeze through the revising part. Take your time. Get some beta readers to look at your work. Let the book rest for a month, then read through it again. Don't rush!

4. You're going to be met with a lot of rejection, so be prepared.

This is honestly the part I was least prepared for. I knew there would be rejection. I knew my first book might not be the one that made my career blossom.

But if I had known back in 2010 just how much rejection I would be faced with over this decade of writing, I'm not sure I would have ever written a single sentence.

I like to think I've been rejected far more often than the average writer. As I said before, I queried eight of my novels before signing with a literary agent. Of those eight novels, I probably queried 100–150 agents for each one. Therefore, I probably have at least 1,000 to 1,200 rejections from agents, and that doesn't take into account the hundreds of rejections I've had from literary magazines for my short fiction.

Rejection is the name of the game. Some of you will be met with success rather quickly. For others, success might take awhile. You have to let rejection roll off your back. If rejection bothers you, you are going to be in for a world of hurt.

5. Don't self publish your novel because you're afraid of rejection. Do it for the right reasons.

I've heard of writers who send out ten query letters to literary agents, get rejected by all ten, and then quickly self-publish their novels.

I've never understood this method of building a career. If you truly believe in your novel, and you want to go the traditional publishing route, then don't give up at ten rejections. Re-work your query letter. Send your query letter to experienced authors for feedback. Try ten more literary agents. If you're met with more rejections, re-work your query letter again.

If you want to self-publish your novel, then great, but do it for the right reasons, and have a plan. Make sure your novel is edited and that you get a professional cover. Decide how you want to develop your career as a self-published author. I made so many mistakes self-publishing, starting with releasing novels of different genres. Do your research and find what's the best route for you.

6. You might have to query more than one of your books before you sign with a literary agent.

The first novel you query might not get you a literary agent. You might send your query letter to every agent in the world and still be met with only rejection.

Don't sit and stew. Write the next thing. Write something different, something better. The easiest way to fail as a novelist is to write one book, send it out, get rejected, and then give up.

That's not how this works. You need to keep going, keep writing. I could have given up years ago. Think getting rejected across the board for one novel is hard? Try querying *seven* different novels over a six-year period and getting only rejected. Try finally getting about twenty full requests for that seventh novel, and *still* not having a literary agent give you a yes.

Trust me, you have to believe in yourself and your work to make a career out of this. You can't hang your head in shame if one of your novels doesn't work out. Keep going.

7. After you've signed with your literary agent, be prepared to do more drafts of your novel.

The day a literary agent offers to represent you will be one of the best days of your life. It certainly was for me. After seven years of trying, trying, trying, finally I got that incredible e-mail. I was in a state of euphoria for weeks. I thought I had made it, that my time had finally arrived.

This was in April 2017, and here's the deal: signing with a literary agent doesn't mean instant publication, instant fame. Signing with an agent simply gets you one step closer to the dream, a dream that still may be years from your reach. After I signed with my agent, I spent months revising my middle grade adventure novel, in one draft adding 10,000 new words, in another draft adding an entirely new character. I worked on a flashback scene for almost a year than I then ultimately cut.

For me, signing with an agent is where the hard work truly came in as a writer, and you know what? All that work I put into that middle grade novel made me a better writer than I ever thought I could be.

8. When your literary agent submits your novel to editors, you might be waiting awhile.

Here's another sad reality: once your literary agent pitches your novel to editors at publishing houses, be prepared to wait. Unless you're one of the lucky few whose novel gets lots of interest very quickly (and yes, that does happen!), it might take months to get a yes from an editor, or even a year or longer.

It's also quite possible that no editor takes on your manuscript, and then you and your agent will have to begin working on a second project. Again, you can't take these rejections to heart. Even though your novel is now *one yes away* from making your publishing dreams come true, you can't fixate on every rejection that comes in, on every week or month that passes without any word from a single editor.

Definitely stay hopeful every day, but don't obsess to the point where you can't focus on anything else.

9. It might take a decade or longer for your writing dreams to come true.

Again, if I had known at the beginning of 2010 that at the beginning of 2020 I will have written twenty novels but had nothing traditionally published yet, not even an offer from an editor, I probably would never have gotten started.

When I wrote my first book, I genuinely believed it would be published and that, by the end of 2010, if not 2011, I'd have a contract in hand. When I wrote my second book, I thought that one would definitely get me an agent and a publisher. When I wrote my third, the same thing.

It's kind of been that way for ten years running now, and what I've come to learn is basically this…

10. Always, always, always be working on the next project.

Love the process. Love the writing. It's all you can really do in the face of so much rejection.

If you fall out of love with the writing part, it's over. And I've often told myself, especially around 2015 and 2016, when I was starting to wonder if I would ever find any success in my writing, that if I lost the love of writing and storytelling, then yes, it was time to stop.

But that's the beauty of writing, at least for me. The love of it has never slipped away. I wrote my twentieth novel a few months ago, and I had a blast every second writing those characters and that story. It was hard, like every novel is hard, but it was also great fun every step of the way.

If you want to make it as a novelist, you have to always be working on the next project. Don't obsess over the one you just wrote that's now on submission, whether it be the querying process to a literary agent or the submission process to editors at publishing houses. You will drown, I'm telling you. Instead of sitting around and waiting, and worrying, get started on the next thing.

And then one day it will happen. Maybe not tomorrow, or next month, or next year even. But I'm telling you, if you keep it up, and you don't ever give up, all your dreams as a novelist will come true.

3. How to Write Your Novel in a Single Month

You might feel like there's never the perfect time to start writing your novel.

You might feel like there's not the perfect window right now where you'll be able to get it done.

There are so many ways to write a novel. You can write just 200 words a day and complete a novel in about a year or so.

But what if you want to get a first draft of your novel completed quickly and not slowly? What if you could write an entire novel in just a single month?

I'm telling you *it can be done*. More than half of the books I've written in five weeks or less. Five weeks or less, I'm serious!

This is not to say the book is *done* after five weeks. There's still lots and lots of revising to do in the months to come, of course.

But the key to your success as a novelist is being able to write and complete a first draft.

It can be messy. It can be flawed (actually, it *should* be messy and flawed or you're some kind of genius).

But you know what? You will be finished!

And a so-so first draft of a novel is a whole lot more useful than a partially written first draft, or a first draft you've been thinking about for years but have never actually started.

How do you write an entire novel in thirty days or less?

First, figure out a time of day you can commit at least two hours to your novel, three if at all possible. This can be split up into different parts of your day. This can be done all at once, early in the morning, or around noontime, or late at night. Whatever works best for you.

Second, figure out the word count for your genre and decide on a target word count for your first draft. If you're writing a middle grade novel, for example, you should aim for 40,0000–50,000 words. If you're writing a young adult novel, aim for 70,000–80,000 words. For most adult genres, 70,000–80,000 words is the sweet spot, too. Only in science fiction and fantasy should you necessarily aim for more.

Third, do the math. How many words a day do you need to write in order to finish your book in 30 days? If 70,000 words is your goal, you need to get down about 2,400 words a day.

Again, you can split this up if you want. Aim for 1,200 words bright and early in the morning, then another 1,200 words late at night. Figure out what you need to do to make your goal always. Yes, on the weekends, too. You need to commit to this schedule *seven days a week*, not just five or six days a week.

But keep in mind this is only for a single month! Think about that novel you want to write right now. Imagine if your first draft could be done… just *one month* from right now.

You can absolutely write a novel in a single month if you put your mind to it.

Just treat the writing of your novel as a part-time job. Treat it like a new exercise regime. Treat it *seriously*.

The only way this fails is if you get lazy. If you feel sorry for yourself and worry your latest chapter doesn't work. If you miss a day of writing and the next day and ultimately give up.

No matter what, do not give you ever. I've said it before and I'll say it again: you are allowed to screw up often in your first draft.

I've screwed up in the first draft *all the time*. The first draft of my MFA thesis novel in 2017 was such a disaster I had to cut 30,000 words at a later date and rewrite the middle of the book from scratch. That, of course, is worst case scenario. You probably won't have to cut eighty-two pages of writing like I did.

But even if something like that happens, it's okay! Because at least you have the bare bones down. At least you're well on your way to writing a great novel.

I'm currently on the twelfth draft of my MFA thesis novel, and it's far and away the best thing I've ever done. The first draft didn't work as well as it should've, but now, three years and eleven revisions later, the book has developed into something truly special.

The most important thing you can do for your novel writing career… *is write the first draft of your novel*. Don't keep delaying it and delaying it.

So start today and not tomorrow, will you? The world needs your stories. You don't have to slowly and preciously work on the first draft of your book for months and months if you don't want to.

Write it in *one* month instead. I've done it many times before, and you can do it, too.

Just believe in yourself and believe in your story. You can do it!

4. You Can Write Your Novel with Just 200 Words a Day, Too

I write on average 2,000 words a day when I'm drafting a new novel.

I recently drafted a middle grade horror novel (one with a creepy villain ghost!) during a winter break from my college teaching commitments.

How many words a day did I write? About 2,000–2,200 words. Three days I came in a bit short at around 1,800 words. Three or more days I wrote a lot more than 2,200 words.

Why do I write these many words a day? Well, it's what I'm used to. Since I wrote my first novel in 2010, I've always aimed for 2,000 words a day. It's how I've written twenty novels in ten years. It's how I'm able to produce a complete manuscript in a single month.

But here's the ultimate question: is writing 2,000 words or more a day the *only* way to write a novel?

Of course not. Stephen King famously wrote his book The Running Man during one of his spring breaks when he was teaching high school, just one single week. And there are those who manage to write novels strictly on weekends, going five days without writing a single word and then writing 5,000 words or more on the weekend, making for a complete first draft in three or four months.

The truth is you can write your book any way you want. You can write your book 1,000 words a day if you want, not 2,000. If you don't have a lot of time to write, you could even do as little as 500 words.

Or, you guessed it, even 200!

200 words a day, you say? 200 words a day is nothing. It's a paragraph. A few sentences. A few dialogue exchanges back and forth.

You could honestly write 200 words on your lunch break. Or the first thing upon waking up. Or the last thing you do before you go to bed at night. 200 words a day could take ten minutes, maybe twenty. I can't imagine any more than thirty.

But let's say you started a novel on July 1st, writing 200 words a day, every day, all the way until June 30th of the following year. It seems like 200 words day still isn't nearly enough to make enough for an entire novel, but you know what? 200 words a day every day for a full year is *73,000 words*! A superb length for most novels, including adult, including YA. If you're writing a science fiction or fantasy epic, maybe aim for 400–500 words a day. And if you're writing a middle grade, you could probably do as little as 100 words a day.

The truth of the matter is there's no excuse for you not to write your novel this year.

The excuse that "there's not enough time" isn't going to fly. Whether you block out a month of time to write your novel, like I sometimes do, or the summer, when you might have more time off, like I often do, or write it only on weekends, or write a little bit each day, if you have the willpower and drive and a great idea, *you can write your novel*, and you should!

So no excuses. Do it. If you never have any time, start today, or this weekend—soon—and write just 200 words a day, every day. It might seem like nothing for the first month or two, but you'll be surprised how the pages will start stacking up.

5. 10 Things You Can Do Right Now to Improve Your Fiction Writing

1. Write every day.

This should preferably be fiction—whether it be a new novel or short story—but it can be other kinds of writing, too.

Treat writing like exercise. The more you write the more you improve, the same way the more you exercise the healthier and fit you become.

You've never going to get anywhere if you just dabble in writing here and there. Don't just *talk* about writing. Don't endlessly outline a novel or short story project you never begin.

2. Write at the same time every day.

Find an hour or two during your day and commit to writing at that time each and every day.

Again, think of this like exercise. If you're an early bird, write when you first wake up. Write before breakfast. Write before your day has effectively started.

If you're a night owl, write super late. After everyone has gone to bed. After everything has finally quieted down. You might be tempted to watch some TV and get caught up on that latest Netflix show.

If you're serious about writing, you need to skip that hour of Netflix and *work on your writing instead*. You should look forward to that time you have during the day to write.

3. Start reading a craft book about fiction writing.

This is often how I like to start my day. Five to ten minutes reading a really great craft book about writing will give me endless amounts of inspiration.

You close a great craft book ready to do something incredible. You're beyond excited to get back to writing more of your story.

If you have absolutely no idea where to start, find yourself a copy of Stephen King's On Writing and get started today.

Read it slowly. Take notes. Just three to five pages every morning or night will work wonders for your writing, I'm telling you.

Get a fantastic craft book about writing, start reading it today—and see what happens.

4. Join an online writing community.

Writing can often be isolating, frustrating, and really, really hard. You need to do much of this work alone, in your own thoughts, but what will help you considerably in the long run is to find a community of writers you can talk to.

Many people have in-person writing communities. You should definitely look around the area you live in. Even just three or four other writers can make a community.

But something you can do today is join at least one online writing community and introduce yourself.

Find an online writing community, say hi, and tell the community what you like to write and what you're currently working on.

5. Say it out loud, to yourself and to others: "I'm a writer."

This one might seem obvious, but it's harder than you think.

I've written twenty novels, I recently earned my MFA in Creative Writing, and I *still* struggle telling people I'm a writer, and instead will say I'm a teacher because that job brings in a steady paycheck every month.

Right now, forget about that job you may have that brings in the steady paycheck. Sure, you need it to survive. Sure, you might even love that job.

But try this, starting today. Say the words out loud, to yourself first: "I'm a writer." And then say the words to a friend or a family member: "I'm a writer."

And the next time somebody asks what you do for a living, do it, say it, and say it proudly: "I'm a writer!"

6. Buy a notebook and keep it on you at all times.

On one hand, I do believe that the very best ideas stay with you. The best ideas you don't necessarily need to write down.

But almost daily a tiny nugget of inspiration will hit me at the oddest time, and I'm always thankful I have a writing notebook nearby to jot the idea down.

I currently have three notebooks. One next to my bed. One in my backpack. One on my writing desk. They are all filled with random notes about short story ideas, novel ideas, character bios, to-do lists, recipes, pretty much anything you can think of.

They are not organized the way I'd like them to be. It's definitely not easy to find that idea I wrote down two months ago.

But it's *there*. And I can always go searching for it whenever I want.

Notebooks are super helpful for your writing. They are important to have around, trust me.

If you're serious about writing, you should absolutely have at least one notebook with you at all times. And you should try to write in it at least once a day if possible.

7. Read at least an hour a day—in a variety of genres.

Reading is simply an essential practice for anyone who wants to be a writer. Reading is the way you learn how others do it. Reading is the way you learn what works and what doesn't.

And of course, reading is a total blast. Even though I have been writing pretty much every day for the past ten years, I'm in no way sick of the written word.

So read, and read often. Try for one hour a day. At least thirty minutes will work. I like to read in the morning because it's always a nice way to start the day, but any time will work, really.

And don't just read one kind of thing. If you write mystery fiction, don't only read mystery fiction (although you should definitely read a lot in whatever genre you write in).

Read a mix of adult literary fiction, MG and YA fiction, and non-fiction. Read what you want!

You'll never be a great writer if you don't ever read anything.

8. Watch one film every day.

The same way reading is important in your writing life, I absolutely believe with my whole heart that watching films (and television, too!) can help you as a writer.

I try to watch one movie every day. Lately it's probably five films per week. What's great about watching a movie (besides being one of the great ways to truly relax, in my opinion) is that you can always find at least one writing takeaway from any movie you watch.

Great films, good films, mediocre films, terrible films. Doesn't matter.

There's *always* something about the storytelling or the characters or the pacing or the themes that you can transfer to your writing. I've been watching films like a writer for years, and what's so great about doing this is that you can still watch the movie *as a movie*. You can still chow down on your popcorn and enjoy yourself.

But at the same time, you can analyze elements of the movie you can then use later for your writing. And you can have fun while doing it!

9. Find one or more writing partners you can share your work with.

One of the best things you can do for your writing career right now is find at least one writing partner you can share your work with. Your short stories. Your novels.

Your poetry. Your non-fiction. Whatever it is that you write.

Find somebody you can rely on who will be *honest* with you. Not someone who will read your latest draft and say, *it's really good, I don't think you need to fix anything.*

Recently five amazing beta readers agreed to read my MFA thesis novel, and they all gave me pages and pages of super helpful feedback. This part of the process helped me make that novel better considerably.

Having at least one writing partner will keep you on track, keep you energized, and will in the long run improve your writing, I guarantee it.

10. Submit your work constantly.

I've always been a big believer in submitting something every single day. A query letter of your novel to a literary agent. Your latest short story. An older short story. A poem. An essay. *Whatever.*

Submitting constantly will help you as a writer for a number of reasons.

- **First,** submitting work all the time gives you more opportunities to be published or to sign with a literary agent. Submitting every day brings with it all sorts of potential. Every time you get a new e-mail, it might be a piece of great news! It might be someone saying, *hey, we like this, we want to publish it, we want to represent you.*

- **Second,** submitting work all the time will make the rejections sting a little less. When you have so much floating out there in the world—say, fifty query letters to a novel, seven short stories, and three poems, all at the same time—the rejections pouring in won't matter to you as much because there are simply so many more editors and agents you haven't heard from.

- **Third,** submitting work all the time will inspire you to write more. Instead of obsessing over one thing for months—say the revision of your latest novel or the latest short story you've penned—you will already be onto the next project, writing the hell out of something new and fresh while that last project is out on submission. You'll keep writing every day, and that's always the schedule you should stick to if you want to be successful.

So don't be afraid to send out your work! You'll never get anywhere in your career if you keep your stories and novels in the drawer forever.

6. Why You Need to Set Deadlines if You Want to Finish Your Novel

I believe in two things to completing the first draft of a novel.

One, being consistent in your writing schedule, and two, setting a deadline for your completion date and sticking to it!

To me, the deadline is just as important as the daily word count. The deadline starts off way in the future, usually six to ten weeks or so, and when you start writing your novel, it feels like you'll never make it to that final day.

In the summer of 2017, when I started writing my MFA thesis novel the first week of June, my deadline date of Friday, August 11 seemed *impossibly* far away. I wondered if I'd survive this dark, intense story over the course of ten long weeks. And there were moments, especially in late July, when I wondered if I'd come out of my cave in one piece. This was the hardest novel I've ever written. It was the most challenging and ambitious by far.

But after ten weeks of working hard five days a week getting in my words, giving each scene my all, suddenly August 11 appeared, and I typed THE END. It was my eighteenth novel, and yet the feeling of finishing that one was like anything I'd ever experienced. It wasn't just another novel. It was my MFA thesis. It was a story I'd wanted to tell for *thirteen years*. And it was done. Something that'd existed only in my head for years was finally down on paper.

So your first step, the most crucial step in my mind, is writing your first draft, and *completing it*.

Not writing part of it, then leaving a chunk of writing for months down the road. Not writing a 30,000-word first draft that you'll lengthen at a later date.

You need to get a word count down in that first draft that is at least close to the desired word count of your genre. I mostly write YA, so I always aim for 80,000 words. Some of my first drafts come in shorter than that, but 80,000 words is always the ballpark I try for because I'm much more of a cutter in revision. I like to trim down, not build up.

What you need to do, ultimately, is finish your novel. There are no ifs, ands, or buts about it. I suggest you start with your chosen word count. 2,000 words a day is standard. That's what I have done on each one of my novels. If you have the time, and if you think you can do it, aim for 2,000. But 1,000 works well, too. Or 500. Or even 200.

Pick what you feel comfortable with. Pick what you know you'll stick to. If you start at 2,000 words a day and you keep coming up short, you might get frustrated, so if that's the case, go shorter if you must.

Whatever word count you choose, you want to stick to it, and then, if at all possible, you should set a *firm deadline* for the completion of your draft.

This has been a fairly easy task for me because at 2,000 words a day, five days a week, that always makes for eight weeks until my deadline. 10,000 words a week. For eight weeks. So I just pick that Friday on the eighth week.

And you know what I do next? I grab a Post-It, write in black sharpie the deadline date, and I stick it on the corner of my computer monitor so that it's always there. I see it every day. I don't stare at it to give myself anxiety, but to just give myself that daily reminder, the energy really, to keep going and keep meeting my daily word count goals to reach the deadline.

Now, and this is also important: you can finish your draft *before* the deadline. I have done this many times before. I did actually finish my MFA thesis novel on the exact Friday of my deadline in the summer of 2017, but the summer before that I wrote a YA thriller that I finished a whole week ahead of schedule.

This happens. Don't panic if you finish your novel early. And don't try to fill up those remaining days with new filler scenes. Celebrate early! Use those few days you planned to write to instead sleep in, plan other projects, relax. I'm always thrilled when I finish two or more days early.

But by all means, try if at possible to finish your manuscript on the deadline you set for yourself.

Even if the deadline is totally made up. Pretend it's not. Pretend your deadline date is the day your manuscript is due to the editor, is due to a million fans who have requested to read it *that very day*!

I've talked to a couple of people who said this doesn't work because deep down they just know the deadline is bogus, so they forget about it. You can't be like that. You have to treat the deadline seriously, like it exists. Trust me on this.

If you want to finish the first draft of your novel, you need to do two things. Stick to a word count every day, the *same* word count. And set yourself a deadline for the completion of the novel. It can be made up. It doesn't have to be real. But treat it like it is.

And one day, either that deadline day, or soon before, you will have a finished novel!

7. Why Talent isn't Enough to be a Successful Writer

What does a writer need to be successful?

Here's the thing: I've been writing my whole life, and I've always felt I had a talent for it. Not everything I've written has been great, or even good. I've improved as a writer over the years for sure, and a lot of that improvement has to do with my undying determination to be successful.

A lot goes into the career of a fiction writer. Years of hard work. An understanding of the publishing industry. Friends and teachers that give valuable feedback. An MFA program in creative writing (if you think it will help). Lots and lots of luck. And yes, talent.

It's definitely true that some talent is necessary.

Talent is important if you want to be a writer, but sometimes it's hard to diagnose if you actually have any talent. I, for example, do think I'm talented at a few key things in writing. I'm talented at coming up with high-concept ideas that lend themselves to film and television adaptations. I'm talented at setting deadlines for myself and sticking to a schedule, whether I'm writing the first draft or revising later drafts. And I'm usually talented at recognizing what's working in those subsequent drafts and what isn't.

But would I consider myself a *talented writer*? I think I have enough talent to continue, to keep trying. Because at the end of the day, talent itself will only get you so far. You can be the most talented writer in the universe, but if you don't work hard at it, if you don't plant your butt in the chair every day and spend some time writing a new scene, a new chapter, then where does that talent get you?

Is talent all you need?

I believe to be a writer talent is important, but it's only part of the game. Writing and reading every day will get you a long, long way, even if you only have a smidgen of talent.

If you happen to be one of the lucky ones and have loads of talent for writing, and you work hard, you *will* be at the top of the heap for sure. Many people love to write, but only a few have any significant talent for it. If you do have it, congrats, and hopefully you take advantage of that blessing.

But what if you don't think you're talented?

If you don't believe you have a ton of talent, don't fret. Write and read every day, and you will get better. I've been at this almost every day for ten years and I still don't have a traditionally published novel in the world yet. But I'm getting closer to the dream, and it's not because of my talent, of which I may or may not have a lot of.

It's because of years of hard work. And the determination to never give up.

8. Why You Need to Understand Your Market as a Writer

Of course your craft is important as a writer.

For most of us, it's what we pay most attention to, and for good reason. You're never going to get anywhere if your writing sucks. If your writing doesn't come together in the way it should. If your writing is mediocre to the extent that you can never find a literary agent or get any of your work published.

In the beginning, you absolutely should focus almost completely on the *quality* of your writing. Because it often takes a few manuscripts to get really good at it. Nobody but the geniuses of the world write a perfect book the first time around. I've written twenty books in less than ten years, and I genuinely don't feel like I started getting good at novel writing until book twelve or thirteen.

And this is something you should remember, too, before we discuss the importance of writing to the market: *write whatever the hell you want to write.* Write the story, the characters, that mean something to you. Often the best work comes from the heart, and not from some hidden agenda to write something in a popular genre that sells well. Don't resist a story because you think it doesn't fit inside the perfect market or the perfect mold.

If you believe in something, go for it no matter what. Maybe it will fail in the long run. I've had plenty of novels I believed in that failed in the past decade. But maybe if you take a huge chance you'll have a big payoff down the road like you could never believe!

So work on and study the craft of writing, keep practicing with different stories and different characters and different genres if you can, and always write the narratives that compel you the most.

At the same time though, at least eventually, you need to develop a serious understanding of the market you intend to sell your work in.

The word market of course is heavily linked to the word genre, so you might think of it a potential market as readers of adult romance books or readers of adult mystery books.

But market doesn't *always* mean genre. Children's books, also known as kidlit, is a market, not a genre, and going more specific, there's a market in children's books for picture book readers, chapter book readers, middle grade readers, and young adult readers.

Middle grade is not a genre, and young adult is not a genre. Middle grade and young adult are categories, audiences, *markets*.

I write for both middle grade and young adult markets. Although both markets rest in the world of kidlit, these two markets are extremely different. There are different rules, expectations, ages of readers. And the earlier I learned exactly what kinds of stories worked best for these markets, the more success I've had in the last few years as a novel writer.

So how do you develop a better understanding of your market?

There are lots of ways! And don't feel like you need to understand everything right away. It might take a few years and lots of research and exploration to figure out your market to its full potential.

But here are five things you can do right now…

1. Read as many books as you can from the market you're interested in writing for.

This is the most obvious one of course. You should be doing this already. Part of the job of being a writer is being a reader too, and something you should always be doing is reading books, recent ones if possible, that are aimed at the market you're currently writing for.

As an MG and YA writer, for example, I try to seek out the latest and greatest MG and YA books to read. Doing so is fun, first and foremost, but I also learn a little bit from every new MG and YA book I pick up. I learn more about voice, about pacing, about structure, particularly when it comes to books aimed at these two particular markets.

So no matter what market you're writing for, pick up at least one new book a month written for that market and read it cover to cover to try to learn something new.

2. Study what literary agents represent books in that market.

I genuinely believe the earlier you start putting together a database of literary agents that sell books in your market the better. When I was doing revisions on my first novel back in the summer of 2010, I started a Word document of all the potential agents I could send the book to, and then over the course of *seven years* I kept adding to and refining that list, particularly when I moved on to strictly writing for the MG and YA markets. As of 2020 I have an immense twenty-five-page document filled with information about literary agents who represent MG and YA authors.

Knowledge is power, especially when it comes to the world of literary agents, because they are your guides to potentially selling your book to editors. The more you learn about literary agents in your field, the better off you'll be.

3. Research what kind of editors publish book in that market.

This list is a bit more difficult to put together than the list for literary agents, but a great resource you should take a look at if you haven't already is querytracker.com. This site is where you can find everything you need to know about literary agents, as well as most editors, too! Many editors won't look at a query for your novel if you don't have an agent, but some editors will, and even the ones who don't you should begin to learn about.

Yes, at the end of the day, your literary agent will do the hard work of finding what editors they want to pitch your novel to, but it doesn't hurt to at least have an understanding of the big and small publishers out there, and any editor who might be the perfect fit for your latest work-in-progress.

Something I love to do, and something you should do as well, is turn to recent books you love written for your market of interest and read through the *acknowledgements* page at the back! Here you will often find the name of the author's literary agent and editor and publishing house. You can learn so much about your intended market from an acknowledgments page, never forget that.

4. Look up what kinds of books are selling in your market through websites like Publisher's Marketplace.

Another awesome resource for authors is Publisher's Marketplace. You have to pay to join, but it's well worth it. Here you can find what novels are selling and by whom and for how much in any market you choose. I love to see, for example, what's currently selling in MG and YA.

You can keep developing your database if you want, not just of literary agents and editors but also of authors writing in your market. Track the different stages of their novels. Study what that author is doing to get people interested in their novel. I love to see what people are doing and saying on Twitter in the weeks or months before their book's release, for example.

All of this will help you in the long run, even if you might not get your book published for another five years or longer. The more you learn about the publishing industry, the more power you'll have when you finally get your book deal!

5. Take note of ways writers find fresh new hooks and voices for books in your market.

Lastly, don't rely on clichés of books from your market that have sold well in the past. Remember that books coming out today were likely sold a year and a half ago or even two years ago. So what editors are buying and what agents are representing *right now* probably is vastly different!

So don't ever feel pressured to write something that was popular this year or last year because that way of thinking will get you nowhere.

It's a tricky balancing act, I know.

You need to know your market well enough so you don't spend a year or longer of your life writing a novel that for whatever reason *won't ever find a place* in that particular market. If you're writing a YA novel, for example, don't have the protagonist be twenty years old and have your second main character be thirteen. The ages of your characters might not seem important, but in YA the ages are especially important! Don't shoot yourself in the foot like that. Learn your market. Learn what's expected.

But at the same time don't just write the same old story that's sold well in years past. You might think you're being smart by writing a story that has sold before and will likely sell again, but at the end of the day, you'll be better served telling a story you're passionate about, that is unique in some way and offers a freshness to the market.

Just learn your market to the best of your ability and keep writing. If you eventually understand your market well, and are writing one fantastic book after another, your time as a published author will come, I guarantee it!

9. Why You Need to Understand Novel Word Counts

Write a novel that's too long for your genre and your age market will mean instant headaches for both you and the people you're pitching the book to. Write a novel that's too short? Not ideal, but still a much better option than going too long.

What's *most* ideal is that the word count of your novel falls within the range of books in your genre and age market that have sold before. You don't have to hit the magic number. There never really *is* a magic number.

But you should fall within a desired range whenever possible, especially when your book is polished and ready to go on submission to agents or editors.

From what I've gathered from writing novels and querying them to agents, along with research I've done online, here are some guidelines you should follow for word counts…

Adult Literary Novels (70,000–110,000)

For a typical adult literary novel, you're looking at a range anywhere between 70,000 words and 110,000 words. Adult novels I would argue has the largest range, in that you could make the case for shorter works (*The Road* by Cormac McCarthy is only 58,000 words) and novels that go way above the high end (*The Time Traveler's Wife* by Audrey Niffenegger is 155,000 words).

But if you're an unpublished author querying an adult novel to literary agents, I guarantee you that anything less than 70,000 words and anything over 110,000 is going to raise some eyebrows, and not in a good way. Querying your adult novel at 140,000 words will eliminate probably ninety percent or more of the agents you're querying. Querying your adult novel at 52,000 words will also make a literary agent think you haven't done your homework.

I've written three adult novels but have only queried one of them. Each of the three revised and polished manuscripts came in between 75,000 and 85,000 words. The perfect number you should aim for, at least in a first draft, is 90,000 words, and then you can revise the work to your liking, making it shorter or adding more.

I've said it before and I'll say it again: you should try to keep the book under 100,000 words when you get to the querying stage. You don't want to scare away agents, and remember, you can always add to the book later after you've signed with someone.

Science Fiction and Fantasy Novels (90,000–130,000)

The big exception to the "never go over 100,000 words" rule is if you're writing science fiction and fantasy novels, especially for adults. Since you are creating entire worlds from scratch, you are *meant* to go longer in these genres, and anything less than 90,000 words might be looked at with concern. I'm sure 85,000 words is probably OK, but once you start dipping under 80,000, you're probably too short.

110,000 words or so seems to be the magic number for science fiction and fantasy. *The Martian* by Andy Weir comes in at 104,000 words, although *Ready Player One* by Ernest Cline comes in a lot longer at 136,000 words. Again, don't feel scared to query if your fantasy novel is 120,000 words and you feel like you've cut everything you can, but at the same time, don't query your fantasy novel if it's at 200,000 words either.

Mystery & Thriller Novels (70,000–110,000)

At the low end of this genre for adults is cozy mysteries, which clock in around 70,000 words, and at the high end are more literary adult thrillers that clock in well above 100,000 words. One of my favorite thriller novels of recent years, Gone Girl by Gillian Flynn, is a whopping 145,000 words. And the recent bestseller *The Girl on the Train* by Paula Hawkins is 101,000 words. I think your best bet for mystery and thriller novels is something around 90,000 words.

Romance Novels (70,000–100,000)

Romance novels typically come in between 70,000 and 100,000 words, although of course there are exceptions. Nicholas Sparks' *The Notebook* is only 48,000 words, while

Kristin Cashore's *Graceling* comes in at 115,000 words. But for the most part, aim for anything between 80,000 and 90,000 words, at least for the first draft. Notice, for example, that Sparks' novels became a lot longer after *The Notebook*, often reaching 80,000 words or higher.

Young Adult Novels (60,000–90,000)

Okay, now it gets a little tricky. I've been writing young adult fiction for ten years now. I've queried YA novels as long as 92,000 words and as short as 58,000 words. You know when I had the most success? When I queried YA novels between 65,000 words and 75,000 words. Again, a little on the shorter end, but also not *too* short. I think anything 60,000 words and up will be fine, while 90,000 and under you're probably OK, although it still might be in your best interest to go below 80,000 words, at least during the querying stage.

What gets tricky about YA is that there's a flood of different genres. Yes, if you're writing a fantasy or science fiction YA, you may be able to go above 90,000 words. Think of *The Hunger Games* by Suzanne Collins, which is 99,000 words, and *Divergent* by Veronica Roth, which is 105,000 words. But still, keep in mind, anytime you go above 90,000 words, you risk alienating more than a few literary agents with that super high word count.

If you feel your story needs to be long, don't make it 65,000 words because you feel like that might get you a better response from agents. By all means, go to 90,000, or even 95,000. But ask yourself, if that novel is sitting at 109,000 words, if you've done *everything you can* to make it shorter. Does it really need to be that long? It's worth asking yourself, and maybe taking another month or two to try to get it to a more reasonable length.

Middle Grade Novels (20,000–60,000)

I have written three middle grade novels to date, two of which I've queried, and one of which secured me a literary agent in 2017. I made a huge mistake when I attempted my first middle grade novel—the first draft came in at 85,000 words, which is way too long.

My second middle grade book I wrote, the one that got me an agent, varied in lengths from its first draft to its latest draft over the course of three years. The first draft was 41,000 words. At its shortest about five drafts in, it was 34,000 words. At its longest, during a heavy revision process with my agent, I got it up to 45,000 words. The draft that was submitted to editors is 43,000 words. I think 43,000 words is a solid length for a middle grade novel, one that's long enough to tell a complete story with lots of detail and character development.

But you can definitely go longer than that. My third middle grade novel came in at 60,000 words for its first draft and is now at 56,000 words after its second draft.

Middle grade can go as low as 20,000 words for younger MG readers (think *The One and Only Ivan* by Katherine Applegate, which is 26,000 words) and then reach 50,000 words and up for the older MG readers (think Escape from *Mr. Lemoncello's Library* by Chris Grabenstein, which is 47,000 words). There is the occasional exception like *Wonder* by R.J. Palacio, which is 73,000 words. But it's absolutely in your best interest to get your middle grade novel below 60,000 words before you query.

—

To Conclude

Make your novel as long as it needs to be, while at the same time keeping it in the range of your genre and age market. You can shout to the rooftops all you want that your novel has to be 160,000 words, but *nobody will ever hear you*. Feel free to go to the lower end or the higher end of the range, but don't fall or rise completely outside of it.

At the end of the day, you want to get your novel published, don't you? The world needs your stories. Don't make a stupid mistake like the wrong word count to prevent them from reaching the masses.

10. How to Choose the Best POV in Your Fiction Writing

There's so much you have to think about before you begin a new fiction writing project.

You have to think about your characters, your setting, your tone, the market you're writing for. You have to think about how you're going to keep the work compelling and entertaining for your reader at all times.

You know what you also have to figure out? What Point-of-View to use.

Are you going to tell this story in first person (using I)? Or is third person going to suit the work better (using him or her)?

What about multiple points-of-view? Can we see the story from two or more characters? Why or why not?

These are all questions you need to ask yourself before you write a single word of the manuscript because making

---

43

the wrong choice in this department is often a fatal mistake you can never recover from.

So what are the advantages and advantages of each? Let's take a look…

1. First Person

Advantages

- First person helps build intimacy between your character and reader (often a reason why so many middle grade and young adult novels are written in first person).
- You are never *wrong* in the first person. Since you're seeing the events through one person's eyes, what you're seeing is the experience of that person and so there's no wrong way to think or feel.
- The choice for a first person point of view tells the reader *whose story it is*. The reader understands who to root for on page one.

Disadvantages

- Here's the big one—since the reader is seeing the story through only one pair of eyes, the reader can't see different perspectives and be in different places than the protagonist.
- It's harder to develop the other characters of the story since you can only learn of them and see them through your protagonist.
- The voice needs to match the main character's personality. If, for example, you're writing in the first person of a fifteen-year-old, you can't write long passages of literary description, as the fifteen-year-old probably wouldn't think that way.

2. Third Person

Advantages:

- It's the most familiar POV choice. When you're in doubt, usually third person is the way to go.
- You have more freedom as a writer (this is something my MFA advisor taught me about third person). The narrator (you, the author) and the protagonist are two different people. You can *comment* on your protagonist rather than just see everything from the protagonist's point of view.
- Third person is less claustrophobic in a sense because you're not stuck in one person's head the whole time. You can hop around to different places and be more free to experiment as a writer.

Disadvantages:

- One problem with third person is that the characters are always at arm's length. You might struggle helping your reader build empathy for the characters because of this.
- It's more difficult to have an unreliable narrator, since the writer would have to lie, not the actual character.
- You also have to deal with clumsy pronouns. When writing a long scene with a ton of characters, it's hard to keep track of every "he" and "she."

3. Multiple POV

Advantages:

- The most obvious advantage is that using multiple POVs allows you to open up the world of your story.

- Multiple POVs can create a wonderful level of richness and complexity to your writing.
- You constantly keep the readers on their toes and maintain something fresh and interesting in the narrative.
- Going back and forth between characters can build suspense as well.

Disadvantages:

- The main one? It's really, really hard. Each POV character's voice needs to be easily recognizable, and that can be difficult to maintain.
- Your manuscript needs to have logical rules about *when* the POV shifts between characters occur (typically each chapter with a character heading) or the reader will be disoriented.
- It is especially difficult to establish deep emotional connections in multiple POV. If your reader only cares about some of your POV characters and not all of them, they might not fully engage with the story.

So which one do you choose?

You should go with the one that best serves the story you're writing. Think about what you're setting out to do. What do you want to accomplish with your characters, your pacing, your theme, your voice? Which POV would get all of that across the *best*?

I often tell writers who have no idea to go with third person, it's the safe choice, and it's one you can do the most creative work in.

First person is a solid choice for middle grade and young adult, but keep in mind the voice has to come through in a way that's engaging and memorable for the reader.

Multiple POV is a choice you should only make if you're ready for a challenge. You have to implement every strength you have as a writer, and you need a really strong reason for doing it.

Sometimes the choice is instinctual. Sometimes you just know. Other times you might have to write a chapter or two to see. Write a few scenes and then decide if you need to make a POV change.

And then of course there's *second person*, which I feel creates a wonderful mood and quality in a short story but is near impossible in the novel form. Once again, only go with second person if you have a strong reason for doing it and are up for quite possibly the biggest writing challenge of your life.

Whatever point-of-view you end up choosing for your latest work, I wish you all the best!

11. How to Choose Between Present Tense and Past Tense

Before you start a new fiction writing project, you also have to pick a tense.

Picking a tense is hard because there's not necessarily a correct answer. There's not always the obvious choice to make.

The same way you have to decide the POV of your book, you have to decide if you're going to write it in past tense or present tense. This is not a choice to pick at random. You want to think carefully and critically because the wrong decision can make for major headaches later.

Maybe the most famous use of present tense is in *The Hunger Games* by Suzanne Collins. First person, present tense, you are with Katniss every step of the way at the exact moment everything is happening to her. You feel like you're right there alongside of Katniss from the first page to the last. It's a thrilling adventure, in part, because the novel is written in present tense and not in past tense.

Present tense can be a fantastic choice for your latest story or novel. Here are the main advantages…

- The immediacy, first and foremost. The immediacy of the present tense allows us to convey a character's change *as it happens*, not after the fact. In present tense, we are there with the narrator as they change, and hence the story's climax is often more intense and exciting.
- Present tense often feels more cinematic, like a film slowly unfolding before us.
- The present tense also lends itself to exploring doubt and uncertainty, since the events haven't happened yet and thus anything can happen to your characters.

But present tense definitely has its disadvantages, too…

- Present tense restricts our ability to manipulate time. It seems natural to alter the chronology of events in past tense, when the narrator is looking back, but it seems unnatural to do it while the events are happening *right now*.

- Sometimes present tense isn't as suspenseful as past tense because there can be a lack of urgency to the storytelling.
- The use of present tense also encourages the writer to include *trivial events* that serve no plot function simply because such events would actually happen in the naturalistic sequence of time.

That last disadvantage is something to think about if you write your latest project in present tense. Are you going to describe every trivial event that happens? Are you going to tell us everything your character does?

Ultimately you're going to want to pick the tense that works the best for your story.

And you know what? Sometimes you won't know right away. Sometimes you make an intelligent guess and then soon discover you made the wrong choice.

This has happened to me before. In twenty novels I have made mistakes about tense, and POV too, and have had to start over from scratch. Sometimes you feel super confident about a tense, but then you read those first three chapters back and realize the tense should be changed. If this happens, don't panic. Just do what's right. Make the changes that are needed.

And if you have no idea what tense to choose, *go with past tense.*

It's more classic. It's more common. When it comes to the gatekeepers like literary agents and editors, they'll probably be happier to see past tense rather than present tense. Present tense isn't for everyone, after all, while pretty much everyone is on board with past tense.

But if you want to give present tense a try, by all means, do it! I love present tense, writing it and reading it. If you're not sure if you'll be successful at it, write a short story in present tense and see how it feels.

To grow as a writer you have to take chances and keep learning new things. You'll want to eventually try both tenses in the long run, but for now pick the tense that feels right for your latest project, and then focus on what you should always be focusing on—telling a great story.

12. Why You Need to Push Past Fear as a Writer

Fear is something that can affect your writing life a lot.

It's affected me in every novel or screenplay or short story I write, absolutely.

Fear is everywhere, and it strikes us all at different times, in different ways.

But what's probably scarier than anything for the life of an artist is staring at that blank page.

There are definite pros and cons to the blank page, of course.

I find what's most exciting about the blank page is the sense of possibility. You have a completely new opportunity to write something glorious.

You also have the opportunity to produce utter crap, maybe something that will be discarded down the road.

But for today? You get to play. You get to write the scene you have in your head the best way you can.

If it works beautifully, then fantastic. Good for you. You'll have less revision to do later.

If it doesn't work, you get to come back another day and try again. You can keep some of what you wrote, or most of it, or none of it. It's entirely up to you.

What's the biggest negative of the blank page? Fear.

The truth is you have to move past it… and write your novel anyway.

I firmly believe if you have zero fear starting a new writing project, you're probably doing it wrong. If you just sit down and know your story and pound it out in a way you think is perfect, with no fear at all, I would be surprised if it turned out to be any good.

Because fear is necessary as a writer, the same way it's necessary for an actor taking on a role he or she isn't sure about, or a painter who wants to try a different style or method.

I've written so many books now that if I take on a new story I feel totally comfortable with, it's not really worth doing. I want to be scared. I want to be unsure. I want to try something different, always.

Fear is necessary at first, but then you need to step past that fear and start writing and see where the day's work takes you. It's all you can do.

And then, once you get going, do whatever you need to do to let go of that fear.

—

You'll have time to revise later. You'll have people months down the road tell you this chapter doesn't work or this character needs more development, or whatever.

For the purpose of the first draft, commit to the story you want to tell, push past the fear, and write it the best you can.

Don't worry so much. Don't stare at that blank page for thirty minutes in terror at what you might screw up.

Don't be afraid to screw up. The only thing that matters is that you get your story down, that you finish what you started.

Let fear play a role in your writing life, but don't ever let it consume you. And then you'll be well on your way to a project you can be proud of!

13. Why You Should Know What You're Doing as a Writer

When you read a book, you hope the writer of that book knows what they're doing.

When you put on a movie, or a new television show, you want to believe the writers and directors knew what they were doing, too.

And when you begin a new writing project, you yourself should have a clear idea of what you're doing and where you're going.

This is not to say you won't make mistakes. There will be plenty of them.

I make hundreds of mistakes on every novel I write, and I always feel bad when I reach the end of my first draft, or even a revision, and the book still isn't anything close to the original vision I had of it.

The point of a first draft is to tell yourself the story, to get the story down as best you can. The point, really, of a first draft is to *finish it*, not to make it perfect, not to make it seem like you know exactly what you're doing all throughout the process.

If you start the first paragraph of a novel thinking you know exactly what you're doing every step of the way, you probably won't even finish the first chapter, let alone the entire novel.

The problems arise when your finished book is in the hands of readers, and the readers feel like you, the author, had no idea what you were doing.

Why do they feel this way?

The readers might find sentences and paragraphs that don't work, sure.

But for the most part, the reader will think you didn't know what you were doing if the story *doesn't lead anywhere interesting.*

Haven't you ever watched a movie, liked it fine for its first half, maybe its first two-thirds, but then realized in the end the writer and director had no idea what they were doing the whole time and delivered an ending that makes zero sense?

Worse is when this happens with a television series. You've invested six seasons of your time, maybe more. Hundreds and hundreds of hours. And then you reach the final season, and the last episode, and *womp womp*. The whole thing ends with a whimper. You realize there was no grand plan. They were truly just making it up as they went along.

Take that anger you've likely felt before, and channel it into making sure your writing *never* delivers that kind of feeling for any of your eventual readers.

One easy way to do that is to figure out exactly what you want to say in your story.

Again, you'll make mistakes. You might get the ending wrong the first time out, maybe even the second time out. I've had to re-write my endings before, and, almost always, the endings are ultimately made better.

Don't ever stop working on a novel until you feel it's ready. This could be a fifth draft. This could be a tenth draft. Never feel like your novel is ready because it's good *enough*. Make sure the novel is the best it can possibly be.

There will be readers who love your story. There will be readers who hate your story. But you always, always, always want your reader to *finish* your story and not put it down halfway through because they get the sense that you, the author, had no clue what you were doing.

Do the necessary work to make sure that never happens.

14. Don't Panic if You're Not a Successful Writer Yet

I wrote my first novel at age twenty-five.

A few months before I turned twenty-six, I had that first novel on submission to literary agents, and I was writing my second novel, my first young adult book called *Happy Birthday to Me.*

And I felt on top of the world. Thought for sure within the next few months big things would be happening.

And although I knew even then that I might not actually have a book published for another year or two, I was certain I'd be published before I turned… gasp… *thirty.*

Everything was going to work out. Everything was going to be just fine.

Well, here I am now. I'm a few months away from turning thirty-six, and I still have no books traditionally published in the world yet.

And you know what? That's okay to me.

Someone else, especially a person in their early twenties trying to make it as a novelist, might say that age thirty-six feels really, really old to not have a first published novel.

But this is how I look at it. I would be sad, disappointed—mortified!—if the first or second book I wrote had been the one to be traditionally published.

You know why? Because I wasn't ready yet. My talent wasn't there yet. My skill wasn't honed.

In the past decade, I've had not only tons of writing experience, but I've earned an MFA in Creative Writing and my MFA thesis novel I recently completed is night and day better than anything I've written.

I've learned so, so much. And I feel more confident than ever now as a writer of fiction.

The truth is, getting an agent, getting published, will take longer for some of us.

You occasionally hear about that young author who gets a six-figure publishing deal, and we all hang our heads in shame feeling sorry for ourselves.

Stephen King was worried when his first few novels didn't sell that he might *never* get a book published and instead remain a high school English teacher for the next forty years with some unpublished manuscripts in the drawer he tinkers with from time to time.

He was—get this—twenty-six when his first book *Carrie* was published. So he was only in his mid-twenties when he was genuinely worried about his publishing future.

On one side of the coin, there's Veronica Roth, whose hit young adult novel *Divergent* was published when she was just twenty-two years old.

On the other side is Raymond Chandler, who didn't have his first book published until he was fifty-one.

And then there's Cynthia D'Aprix Sweeney, whose debut *The Nest* didn't come out until she was fifty-five.

I've even read stories about authors in their eighties and nineties who have their first book published.

In the end, all that matters is that you keep going.

The thing is, it's not that important what age you are when you become a published author. Because, at the end of the day, you will be published when it's the right time for *you*. When your talent and skill matches the right book with the right agent and editor.

There's a lot of luck involved, that's to be sure, but time to develop your craft will only benefit you in the long run.

As long as you keep going, you can have the writing career you want, I guarantee it.

I'm okay with not being published until thirty-six or later. And you should, too!

15. Why You Do Your Best Writing in a Place of Your Own

My best work, absolutely, comes when I write in a specific place—the office at the front of my house.

I've written my twenty books in so many different ways. I've written morning, noon, and night. I've written seven days a week, five days a week. I once wrote a novel one week a month for an entire year.

And I've also written them in different settings. When I first started writing novels, I wrote in my tiny bedroom in Los Angeles, sitting down at my desk every night between 10 P.M. and 1 A.M. trying my best to put words on the page. I had a small window in the room, but at night I couldn't see anything outside, so my eyes stayed focused on the computer screen for hours at a time.

When I moved back to Reno in 2011, I wrote a few novels outside my home, often in coffeehouses. There are pros and cons to writing a novel in a place where conversations surround you. The big pro for me, and I know this sounds corny, is that *you feel less alone.*

Writing is a lonely job. You often spend hours a day sitting by yourself in silence. Sometimes it's nice to have people talking around you, and occasionally the amount of noise actually gave an urgency to my writing, especially when I was writing a long scene of dialogue.

But, at least for me, the cons of an environment like this to do your writing outweigh the pros.

A big con is that I'm unable to fully focus on my writing when I have people talking in the nearby vicinity, let alone ten conversations or more surrounding me.

When I'm stuck on a paragraph or a scene, silence helps me figure out where to go next. When there's too much noise, I can't focus. Also, I always feel bad, especially in a crowded coffeehouse, that I've stolen a table for two hours or more.

And while this is a minor issue, I have to say it anyway: when you write in a coffeehouse, eventually you need to *use the bathroom*. And it's really annoying to have to pack up all your stuff, walk to the bathroom (which may or may not be occupied), and then come back to your table to set up all your stuff again. Worse, that table you've been hogging for the past two hours might be taken by the time you return from the bathroom!

I'd say in the past few years, I've only written outside the home when for one reason or another I didn't have the time to get my writing done at home, and I simply had to do my writing somewhere else.

In the past it's been between classes I'm teaching, when I have a two-hour window that's too short to drive all the way home and back and when I should be using every spare minute instead to work on my writing.

Ultimately a place of your own is the *best* place to do your writing.

That can be a number of places. It can somewhere outside your home even, especially if it's a place where you feel you have the best opportunity to create and to thrive as a writer.

For many people, it's somewhere quiet outside. For others, it's a dark room where you can focus for hours on end without ever being interrupted. The bedroom. An office. A basement. An attic. It can be anywhere you want. Just make sure it's your own place.

For me, the place I do my best writing is the office at the front of my house. Since early 2016, I've been lucky to live in a home that has an office completely designed as an ideal writing space. I have a big black desk that faces a huge window. Through that window I can see not only the street and neighboring houses but also a huge mountain in the distance that towers toward the sky.

When I'm stuck in my writing, I love to sit back in my chair and stare at that mountain. It seems cheesy, but sometimes just thirty seconds fixated on it will bring me the idea I need.

I've written on my bed before, and sometimes I write at the dining room table, especially when I'm hungry and like to be closer to the pantry (hey, we all have our weaknesses).

But for the most part, the last five novels I've written have been drafted and revised in that front office, where I can keep the door closed, sit in total silence, focus my mind on the scene I'm going to work on that day. And then, when I finish, I can emerge into the world again.

So if you're serious about becoming a writer, try to find a place of your own to do your work. Find a place that lets you concentrate. Lets you relax.

And yes, lets you dream.

16. Why You Don't Need to Only Write What You Know

We've all heard the advice before: *write what you know.*

I heard it so often growing up, and I still hear it to this day. And even though it's kind of a cliché, there is some validity to the saying.

When you write what you know, you ultimately have expertise in something that not everyone else has. You're able to pull from your experiences and memories to make for fiction that reads truthful from beginning to end.

For example, I've been teaching at the college level for seven years now. I know that world really, really well. And whenever I set a scene in that kind of setting, I'm able to do it better than someone who might be thirty years removed from college or who's never taught a day in their life.

I've also been writing almost every day for ten years.

Fiction. Essays. Academic writing. Screenplays. So much creative work.

I definitely understand the work of the writer, and what they go through on a daily basis. This is probably why

Stephen King writes so often about novelists in his books. This is why so many writers love to *write* about *writers*.

I have also written and directed short films, more than thirty between the years 2001 to 2009. This is why I've written a lot about filmmakers in my novels, particularly since not a whole lot of filmmakers end up writing novels. I know that world and understand its highs and lows, the sheer rush that comes with the process but also the high risks and odds of major disappointment.

So, yes, it's important *to an extent* to write what you know.

If you take on a novel with characters who work in different professions than your own, who are characters wholly unlike yourself, you're going to need to do some research. You can't just pull everything you write out of your own imagination.

If you're writing about a profession you know little about, it's probably in your best interest to read about it, even speak to one or more people who does it. You don't have an excuse as a writer to just make it up and hope you get it all right.

At the same time, though, the heart and imagination know things, too. So don't just write book after book only about what you know. Free your imagination, and challenge yourself to write about different professions, different experiences. Let your heart guide the way, and then also use whatever research you need to make sure the specific details come across as authentic and true.

Try new things, always. Remember to put in whatever research is necessary.

And never forget to listen to your heart and imagination. It's amazing how far these two things will take you!

17. Why You Don't Need to Have an Outline to Write Your Novel

You read that right. It's not essential that you write an outline for your novel.

Now this is not to say you *shouldn't* write an outline. If you feel more comfortable plotting your book before you begin chapter one, go for it, by all means.

But if you're like me, a pantser as they call it, someone who falls in love with an idea, and maybe a character or two, and soon after begins writing a new novel to see where it goes, then don't under any circumstances feel obligated to write an outline.

In 2017 I signed with a literary agent to represent a middle grade novel called *Monster Movie*, and it was a book I wrote with zero outline, only some specific details about the characters, a clear idea of the beginning and the ending, and some fleeting ideas about what happens in the middle.

An outline can be helpful in your writing. I actually find outlines a necessity when writing a *screenplay*, since that medium of writing is much more structured than novel writing and requires a strict attention to scene length.

But for novels, an outline can oftentimes feel more like a crutch than an ally.

Instead of going somewhere new and exciting with an upcoming scene or trying something with a character you might not have thought of weeks prior, you may feel obligated to follow that initial outline to its appropriate end.

If you write an outline, I suggest you never feel married to it, that you can rip it up and start all over even if you're halfway through the first draft of your manuscript.

If you don't use an outline? Here are the three things you need to write a good novel...

1. Character Biographies, Descriptions, and Motivations

Instead of writing an outline of all the scenes I plan to include in the book, I take a few days and write an extremely detailed biographies about my main three to five characters.

I write down the name, describe him or her physically, jot down notes about the character's history that may or may not show up in the finished novel, and then *in bold* write down what he or she wants and what is preventing him or her from getting it.

These lines in bold I turn to at least once every other day as I'm drafting the manuscript, so I never forget it. What does each character want, and what's stopping that character from getting what they want? It's essential. It's what drives the story forward always.

2. The First Scene and the Last Scene

I never start writing a new novel without a clear and vivid understanding of how the book begins and how it ends.

This is not some vague idea about what the first or last scene entails. It's an extremely specific understanding of what happens at each step of the scene. Typically I've already written both the first chapter and the last chapter *in my head* before I write a single word down for real.

Sometimes, after many revisions, these scenes change. For my agented middle grade book, the first scene never really changed much from its initial draft back in 2015, but the last scene did considerably.

My latest young adult thriller I've been actively revising has an opening scene that ultimately didn't work as well as I wanted it to, so I wrote an entirely new opening scene years later.

For the purposes of the first draft, have a clear idea of where the book begins and ends, whether you've jotted down notes or figured it all out in your head.

It's also helpful to have some ideas of scenes in the middle of the book too, but by no means required.

3. Word Length Goal, a Schedule, and a Deadline

Word counts are important in novels, especially when you're trying to pitch your book to agents or editors in a specific genre that comes with an expected word count range.

For example, if you're writing a young adult novel, you probably shouldn't pitch a book that's 150,000 words when 80,000 words is to be expected.

Lastly, give yourself a schedule and a deadline, and *stick to it*. If you commit to a day you simply must have that manuscript finished, and remind yourself of that day

—

constantly, then you'll have a better chance at succeeding in completing your novel.

So relax. Don't feel like you have to take three weeks to write a scene-specific outline of your novel.

You'll have more room to play without an outline like that, and as long as you instead write detailed character bios, have a clear idea of the beginning and ending of the story, and stick to a schedule and deadline, you'll be able to write a book of the highest quality.

18. Why You Need to Let the Best Ideas Come to You

Where do good story ideas come from?

It's the big mystery. When I think back on all the novels I've written thus far, I realize the kernel of the ideas changes from book to book.

But I've never sought out an idea. I've never surfed the web to find something that *might make an interesting book*. Almost never do I get an idea one day and then start writing the first draft of that novel the next.

Sometimes a good novel idea comes from an experience I recently had, but I've also gotten ideas that came out of nowhere. Sometimes the best ideas don't stem from personal experience or a tale your best friend tells you one night over drinks.

Sometimes a great idea will hurl toward you in a flash, and often the best of these will stick with you for many weeks and months.

—

For me, when the idea doesn't come from experience, it comes to me in an *image.* This has happened multiple times throughout the years.

The best ideas do stick with you more than you might realize.

I think a notebook is important to have so you can jot down details about the story idea you're excited about and give breakdowns for your major characters.

But a drawer of Post-It notes with a thousand story ideas sketched out everywhere?

That's not really useful, because the best ideas will stick with you, and the bad ones will *float away.*

And Lord knows I've had some bad ones over the years that thankfully disintegrated from my mind before I had a chance to develop them further.

The good ones will stay, I guarantee it.

And you'll spend time thinking about where the idea can go, who the main character should be.

The excitement will take over, and then you'll know *that's* the story you should go with.

So if you don't have an idea for your next novel yet, don't panic. Don't go searching for an idea. Don't struggle.

Go about your life, take some walks, clear your head, and something will hit you at just the right time.

It always does for me.

19. Amazing Stories are Created When You Mix Unrelated Ideas

Having one strong idea come to you is great. Having *two* unrelated ideas that are strong and that can be blended into the same story? Now we're talking!

I've always been driven to stories that do something a little different, that take a concept that might feel familiar but then becomes something totally unexpected.

Often I'll come up with one idea. It interests me, but it doesn't excite me. I'll think on the idea for a few weeks, maybe even months. *Hmm*, I'd ponder. I could *do* something with that.

But that's not enough for a novel, or even a short story.

So I'll forget that idea, maybe go on to the next. And sometimes, on the best days, I'll think of a *second* idea, match it with that first one I came up, and whoa—trust me, you'll know when it feels right.

The idea of mixing those two ideas into one story suddenly gets your heart pounding, your mind racing, your imagination bursting.

And remember this, too—blending two unrelated ideas extends to any genre you write in.

Think of it for romance: a man and woman meet and fall in love. Yawn.

But what if you added a second unrelated idea: the woman's younger brother killed the man's previous wife in an accidental hit and run and has been keeping the tragic incident a secret from everyone. Better, right?

Now there's something going on underneath the surface to keep you flipping through the pages. (That example, by the way, was from Nicholas Sparks' *A Bend in the Road*.)

It's not enough to say, okay, I'm going to write a haunted house novel. Delve deeper.

What's an unrelated idea, something unusual, you could bring to the haunted house novel?

If you want, you can even mix more than two unrelated ideas.

Try three. Maybe even four! (But don't try ten. I mixed probably ten or more into a novel once and I think that was about five too much.)

Please, though, be original. Don't just sit down at your laptop and write a science fiction epic that's like *every other* science fiction epic. Think of something new and exciting you can do with your science fiction story.

What could you mix in that would make it different from everything else, that would make it truly soar for readers?

At the end of the day, you want to bring something original to your work.

Even if you write in a specific genre, you want to bring your own personality to your writing at the same time that you blend together at minimum two completely unrelated ideas.

In the long run, your readers will thank you for it!

—

20. A Fresh Take on an Old Idea is More Important than a New Idea

One more thing about finding ideas for your novels…

In the fall of 2014 I took a graduate creative writing course at the University of Nevada, Reno, where we focused on the seven basic storylines we find in pretty much all literature, film, and television.

We read from cover to cover a fascinating book by Christopher Booker called *The Seven Basic Plots*, and he certainly brought up some good points.

What are the seven basic plots?

- Overcoming the Monster (*Beowulf, Dracula, James Bond*)
- Rags to Riches (*Aladdin, Cinderella, David Copperfield*)
- The Quest (*The Odyssey, The Lord of the Rings, Apocalypse Now*)
- Voyage and Return (*Alice in Wonderland, The Time Machine, Gone with the Wind*)
- Comedy (*Much Ado about Nothing, A Midsummer Night's Dream, Four Weddings and a Funeral*)
- Tragedy (*Romeo and Juliet, Macbeth, Bonnie and Clyde*)
- Rebirth (*Beauty and the Beast, A Christmas Carol, Groundhog Day*)

Now think back on the stories you've already written. Any novels you've worked on these past few years. Does your narrative line up with one of those seven basic plots?

It can be a variation on one of the plots. It can be unique and only loosely tied to one of them.

But I'd bet any fiction you write in your life will likely have at least one of those plots, often without you knowing!

Sure, you might think you have no talent, have no imagination, when all the work you've produced to date fits snugly into one of seven plots. But actually, nothing could be further from the truth!

Because a fresh take an old idea and executing it well is your key to success as a fiction writer.

You can spend the next year waiting for inspiration to hit, waiting for that incredible new idea to emerge that no one's ever written before in the history of the world.

You know what? You're probably going to have to wait longer than a year. You might have to wait your *entire life*.

Every story, basically, has already been told. Even the most audacious, most unexpected, most unbelievably creative ideas we see here and there in film, television, and literature, are *still* variations on these old basic plots.

So don't obsess over finding a new idea. Instead, find fresh takes on *existing* ideas you can put your own spin on, give your own voice to.

Don't just write the same old thing with a few small differences, of course. Write something new and fresh that just so happens to be a take on an existing idea. Make your story so dazzling and complex and original that no reader will even consciously realize it's one of the seven basic plots.

What makes every story unique in today's marketplace is the execution of it, remember that. The *how* you tell your story is always more interesting than the story itself.

So don't stress, okay? Don't panic if you think your latest idea isn't new enough, isn't original enough.

If the idea excites you, and there's something awesome you plan to do with that idea, then go for it!

21. This is What It's Like to Start Every New Novel

There's nothing like staring at a blank document when you set out to write a novel. And there's nothing harder, truly, than *actually getting started.* I completed my latest novel in the summer of 2019. And just like all the others, the very first day of drafting the book was by far the most terrifying.

I opened the document and did the easy part: I wrote the title on page one. I'm always pretty good at that part.

Then I scrolled down and typed, CHAPTER ONE. That was easy, too. Then I pushed the RETURN button, and then the TAB button.

And then I saw, gasp, *the blinking cursor.*

This moment is by far the scariest part of writing a novel. Those seconds before you write the first sentence. Partly because I've learned in the last decade how important those first ten pages are if you want to eventually sign with a literary agent and get your novels traditionally published.

Agents and editors are busy people. They don't necessarily want to say no to you, but they also have to be wowed by that opening chapter to continue reading and eventually say yes.

It's sad but true: you can write the best novel in the world, but if chapter one is terrible, you're in for a world of hurt.

The whole book needs to be as great as you can make it, but you always want to wow them with that first chapter, that first *page*, really.

You want to make it clear the kind of book you're writing and showcase a unique and compelling voice right from the start.

Therefore, you might stare at that blinking cursor on day one a long, long time, like I often do. You might write a few sentences, then erase them and start over. You might write a few paragraphs and think they're crap.

It's OK. It happens. Begin writing a couple of times if you need to. Doing so doesn't make you a bad writer. Opening a novel is *hard*, and few of us get it exactly right the first time. That's why revisions are so important.

That's why the revision part *is* the writing to me in a sense, because that's when you actually shape the work chapter by chapter into what you wanted it to be in the first place.

Revisions will come. For now, take a deep breath, and start your novel.

Your first 500 words might totally suck. They might be so bad you want to quit as a writer right then and there.

Keep going anyway. Finish that first chapter, whether it's day one of writing or day two or whatever. Then start chapter two and write some more.

Usually I relax around chapter five. I finally find a decent groove I try to maintain all the way to the end of my book a few weeks later.

No matter what, you have to push past the fear, and *get going with your story*.

Write the opening as best you can, and if it sucks, that's fine! You can fix it later.

I've thrown out and rewritten opening chapters *months* after completing the first draft. Sometimes you have to look at the whole of a novel to see what's working and what isn't working.

But you can't ever see what's working and what's not working when there are *no words on the page*.

So if you're ready to begin writing your novel, begin today and not tomorrow, and realize that the terror you feel is completely normal.

What will make you stand out from the others is actually starting the novel in the first place, and that you keep going every day until you reach the end!

22. Here's One More Thing You Need to Ask Yourself Before You Start Your Novel

There's a lot you need to ask yourself before you begin your novel.

And there's a lot of preparation you need to do, too, of course. Each writer embarks on a writing project differently, but when it comes to a new novel, there are a few things you simply must do.

You should understand the expectations of the genre you're writing in. You should figure out a schedule so that you stick to a word count every day until you reach the end of the project.

You should also spend a long time figuring out *who your main characters are*, what they're all about, what they want, what's keeping them from getting what they want, what their flaws are, how they might change throughout the course of a novel.

I've talked about how you don't necessarily need to write a strict outline to a novel beforehand, that writing down every chapter and scene before you write the first sentence of your book can actually hinder your creativity because there's nothing really to surprise you as you go about your writing days.

But knowing a lot about your characters is a must. Get comfortable with their physical descriptions, yes, but also pay attention to everything else. The more you understand your characters the better the writing will go, I guarantee it. I've definitely learned this the hard way!

So figure out your characters, especially your protagonist, and then ask yourself another big question.

Am I writing a specific story that could only happen to this character, in this world, in this time?

Once you've figured your main character out, now you need to move onto setting and time period. This part might seem simple, might feel like you don't have to pay close attention, but you really should.

Setting of course depends on the genre of novel you're writing in. If you're writing a science fiction story set not on this Earth, you're going to need to spend just as much time with setting as you do with character. What planet does the story take place on? What aspects of Earth will we see and what aspects unlike Earth will be presented?

But funnily enough, sometimes it's even harder to come up with a setting for a realistic literary story. You might be inclined to just use the city you currently live in. I've certainly done that before. You should ask yourself, though, what would change about your story if it was instead set in L.A., or New York, or a small town in North Carolina.

If literally *nothing* changes about your story, you haven't put in enough work yet. There should be something specific about your setting that impacts your story, and how that setting impacts your main character!

Finally, you have to think about the time period of your story. Is there something about your story that makes sense to be told in the past? Five years ago? Fifty years ago? So many beloved and respected published novels are set in extremely specific time periods. Is setting your novel in 2020 your only choice?

Now, you shouldn't ever just pick a random year to set your novel in if you don't have *a really strong reason for doing so*. Don't think you're going to stand out just by setting your novel in 1985 instead of 2020. If you're writing a contemporary story, then by all means, set it now, and make sure it feels like today, and not five or ten years ago.

But if the story you're telling about a specific character and a specific setting would be better suited for a time in the past (or the future!), then, by all means, go for it!

All right, are you feeling ready to begin writing your novel? In the next part we dive into everything you need to do to write your first draft… and write it well!

DRAFTING & STORYTELLING

23. Why You Need to Write Every Day

Do you really need to write every day? The short answer is YES.

People often think I'm joking when I tell them I write every day. I get a lot of responses like, "yeah, okay, sure." It sounds good, but it doesn't seem *realistic*. Sometimes life gets in the way. Sometimes things happen.

But if you want to be a writer, yes, I implore you to write every single day.

Writing every day does not necessarily mean you have to write ten hours a day, or five, or two, or even one. Writing every day is different for everybody, depending on work schedules, depending on family obligations.

Although I wouldn't advise you to only write for, say, *two minutes* a day, it's still, in my mind, a better practice to write for at least ten minutes seven days a week than to write for a few hours just one or two days a week.

What you want to do is think of writing like exercise.

You should think of writing like exercising (or maybe not, if you never work out). For me, I try to exercise for forty-five minutes to an hour five times a week, if not six.

This is rarely a hard work-out. It can be the elliptical, or free weights, or a run with my dogs, or, when I'm really lazy, a walk to the nearby park and back. The key is to do *some kind* of exercise and movement almost every day.

It's the same thing with writing. You want to constantly be practicing.

But wait—do you ever get a break?

Occasionally, sure, you need a break. There were a few years where I wrote three to four hours every day during the week, and then I would take the weekend off. I wrote a few of my novels like that. I would work super hard for five days, then take two days off and not write a word.

But actually, in looking back at those novels I wrote only five days a week instead of seven, there was something missing. No matter how hard I tried to get back into the groove on Monday, it always took me until Tuesday or even Wednesday to find my rhythm again. And the characters tended to get stale at times when I wasn't writing them every day.

So no excuses: the first draft of a novel should be worked on every day until it's completed!

When you're writing the first draft of a novel, work on it every day. It can be a small chunk of your day, that's fine. An hour instead of four hours. 500 words instead of 2,000. Whatever works for you.

But as long as you're living in the world of your story a little bit every day, the characters will start to feel like real people, and your story will come alive for you more and more.

Writing every day allows you to take new chances… and better yourself as a writer. When you finish the first draft, *then* take some time off from writing. You're actually *supposed* to let your manuscript rest for a few weeks so that you come to the second draft with fresh eyes.

But does that mean you shouldn't write anything for four weeks or more? Absolutely not.

Try to find something to work on every week. Revise another novel you've written. Write a new short story, a poem, a screenplay, an essay. Take a risk. Do something outrageous. Try something you've never attempted before.

And then, after some time has passed, get started on the second draft of your newest novel and see that revision through to the end.

If you want to be serious about writing, you need to write every single day, no excuses. Trust me, you won't regret it!

24. Why the Best Time of Day to Write is the Morning

Are you a morning person? I'm definitely not!

I'll be honest: I'm not a morning person. I actually find it really hard to function before 9:00 A.M.

For the most part I've been able to design my life where I haven't had to do much every day before that time, but occasionally I have to leave the house early or have a job that starts at the first sign of daylight, and so I'm forced to make do. I find my brain starts kicking into gear around 10:00 A.M. and often not before.

At the same time, I'm no longer much of a night person either, although I used to be. When I was in my twenties, I stayed up until 2:00 A.M. every night. There's something so magical, so calming, about the night. When everything quiets down, and there's no urgency.

But writing every night can also burn you out fast, and I feel strongly that mornings are the best times for writing.

There is nothing more glorious than getting your 2,000 words down fast early in the day.

Sometimes I start writing as early as 9:00 A.M. Other days, for whatever reason, I don't start until noon. On the occasional day when I didn't plan well, I'm not writing until late into the afternoon.

And here's the deal: I find, almost one-hundred-percent of the time, that the earlier in the day I start my writing, *the better the work is.* When I've been busy all day, and I begin writing late in the afternoon, the work isn't as strong.

There truly is a thrill in finishing your writing early in the day and then having your afternoon, evening, and night to do other things. Maybe revise some of your work. Read a book. Watch a movie. Make a nice dinner. Relax.

I've heard of authors who treat writing like a full-time job in that they actually write non-stop for eight hours, maybe taking a short break for lunch.

I've never been able to do that, and I don't think I ever will. I have, on average, *three good hours* of writing in me every day. Three hours of total concentration and creativity. After three hours, I begin to fade, and then the work suffers, so why bother continuing?

But wait—is it okay to write later, not earlier?

Yes, absolutely. You are of course welcome to write *any time you want.*

Some of you might feel more confident writing at night, and if so, go for it. Some of you might also have work obligations that begin so early that the only way for you to get the words down is to sit at your writing desk later in the day.

Some of you have kids, responsibilities, and it's a fight just to find a thirty-minute window of time to write, let alone those perfect two to three hours in the morning where all your creative juices are flowing. Trust me, I understand.

But if you do have a bit more freedom in your day, consider doing your writing earlier, not later. Try to make mornings the time for your current composition whenever possible. You might find that your writing improves considerably!

25. Pursue Your Writing Projects on the Weekend

—

Correct me if I'm wrong, but I'm pretty sure most people look at the weekend as a time to relax.

To rest and reflect. To enjoy oneself.

Monday through Friday is when you do all the hard work, and Saturday and Sunday is the time to have fun.

But when you're a fiction writer, working project to project, there really is no such thing as a "weekend."

Sure, if you have the luxury of time in your schedule, then by all means, write a lot Monday through Friday, then take the weekend off.

But for the most part, I like to use my weekends not to relax necessarily but to catch up on my work and write even more than I did during the regular work week!

If you have a busy job and a crazy schedule Monday through Friday, and really only have time to write on the weekend, I *still* insist you carve out even just thirty minutes a day Monday through Friday to do a little bit of writing if you can.

Even the slightest bit is still making progress, and you'll end the day knowing you've advanced your project by even that slightest degree. It gives you a sense of accomplishment before you turn in for bed at night.

It should be said that you shouldn't just purge your writing solely on the weekends.

I've known writers who have done this actually. Write nothing Monday through Saturday, then wake up early on Sunday morning and write 5,000 or 6,000 words before noon.

There, that writer says, *voila! I've done my writing for the week!*

As great as you might feel that Sunday afternoon, and while yes, I'd prefer you write 5,000 words one day a week than *zero words* all days of the week, I still don't think this is the best way to write a piece of fiction.

This kind of schedule will burn you out sooner than later, trust me. Writing strong characters, for example, is about living with those characters each and every day.

This is why being consistent is so important, not blocking out one day a week to write a lot of words but rather block out a little bit of time every day of the week to write *some* words.

Having said all this, however, one thing I do recommend, if you have the time to write more on the weekends!

If you only have an hour to write between Monday and Friday, and on most of those days can only get to, say 500 words or so, and then you have your weekend totally open?

No, you don't need to only write for an hour on Saturday and Sunday too, and only get to 500 words.

If you are stretched for time during your work week but always have lots more hours available on the weekend, write more, *lots* more. Write tons! Write 5,000 words a day if you want.

Or write 2,000 words, always my goal when I'm writing my first draft of a novel.

Don't look at your weekend writing as *catching up*. Don't say to yourself, well, I only wrote 500 words a day for the last five days, so now I have to write 5,000 words both Saturday and Sunday to catch up for the week.

Get up on Saturday. Sit at your writing desk. Get your 500 words down.

And now every word you write after that is gravy!

If you want to be a writer, you need to find the time to do the work. If that means an hour or less a day, so be it. If some of your weekends are crazy busy, still try to find that hour to devote to your writing.

But when you have a weekend with hours and hours of free time to do whatever?

Don't completely waste it by goofing off, lounging, bingeing Netflix, avoiding the computer.

Sit down in that chair and write your ass off. You'll be glad you did!

26. Why Boredom is a Good Thing for Fiction Writers

It's so hard to be bored these days.

I remember as a kid being bored here and there, but today there's not really an excuse to *ever* have a single moment's boredom.

All you need to do is turn on the TV and click on one of a thousand options to watch. All you need to do is take out your phone and scroll through Facebook or Twitter.

We do everything we *can* to avoid boredom, don't we? Like, any moment where there's silence, where there's nothing expected of us, we feel awkward.

We simply need to be doing something, always! We can't just possibly sit there, can we?

—

The truth, though, is that boredom is really good for your writing.

There's a reason I like to go for a run almost every day. It's not that running is boring, necessarily. I find running lots of fun, a brief window of escape from my life to get my body moving and see all the sights of my neighborhood, including some cool hidden trails and the gorgeous mountains nearby.

But what running really gets me to do is leave *all the screens behind* so I can have an hour or so to focus entirely on my thoughts. On the ideas that might rise to the surface and inspire a new novel or short story. On the ways I can improve the latest writing project I'm currently working on!

I can't tell you how many problems have been fixed in my work from merely going for a run or a walk and just being a little more bored than usual. Boredom allows for great ideas to come to the surface.

As hard as it may be to do in 2020, even just *ten minutes* of total boredom might actually bring you the immense creativity you need for your day!

Stephen King used boredom to finish his magnum opus, *The Stand*, after all.

There's a story he tells in his craft book *On Writing* that is one of my favorites. He had been working for months on *The Stand*. He had more than 500 pages of writing, so he was too deep in to even think about abandoning the novel.

But he couldn't figure out the third act. He had built up this epic of dozens of characters and didn't have a *clue* how to reach his ending.

So he talks about how he would go on walks by himself every afternoon and try to figure out what to do. The first walk didn't work, and neither did the second.

But one day, while walking, the idea suddenly came to him out of the clear, blue sky.

Pow! There it was! All from letting his mind go blank. All from immersing himself in total boredom.

And he was so scared the idea would slip from his mind that he ran all the way home, eventually out of breath and sweating as he jotted the idea down on a piece of paper.

Boredom in this case not only helped Stephen King with a story problem, but it helped him complete one of his all-time greatest novels.

So lean into boredom. It might actually improve your writing!

When you find yourself with a free half-hour during your afternoon, don't necessarily use that half-hour to catch up on a sitcom you've been watching. Don't use it to scroll through your phone. Don't use it to make a second lunch if you just ate two hours before.

Sure, you can use that half-hour to read—time dedicated to reading throughout your day is *always* important for writers, too. But something else you can do, especially if you're struggling in the first draft of a new novel, or struggling to come up with ideas for the next one, is just sit in a room, in silence, and *bore yourself silly*.

Look around the room and ponder. Close your eyes. Clear your mind. I'm serious about this!

Maybe something amazing will come to you, as it has for me in the past. I know of at least five of my novel ideas that came to me when I was bored and not doing much.

Don't be afraid of boredom. You have no idea the wonders it can bring to your fiction writing.

27. Please Don't Try to be Perfect in Your Writing

I wrote my first novel in 2010, and I wrote my twentieth novel in 2019.

Yep, I have been a writing machine for ten years now. I love to write. I love to practice my craft. I love to think about stories all day and then do my best to tell those stories in novel form.

One thing I don't love to do? I don't try to be *perfect* in whatever I write.

No matter how much better you get in your writing month after month, year after year, you will keep making mistakes. And that's okay.

Mistakes will happen even after you've practiced your heart out.

I felt really good about my nineteenth novel, a middle grade horror book, when I finished the first draft of it in January 2019.

I thought it was maybe one of my best first drafts ever. I let it rest for three weeks, and then I went back to it, and as I worked on my first revision, I kept thinking to myself, *damn, this is pretty good! This is really compelling and flows surprisingly well!*

These thoughts meant something to me because I genuinely *don't* think that most of the time.

I'd say 80% or more of the time when I read the first drafts of my novels I'm trying to keep the vomit down.

This novel I thought *was* working, surprisingly enough. It wasn't perfect. I don't ever strive to be perfect in a first draft. But there was a lot of great stuff in there, and now it was time to shape it and make it better.

But then an important person in my world took a look at it and quickly sent me a big dose of reality.

As it turned out, there were actually a *ton* of problems with the book.

The story wasn't quite convincing. The main character needed to be more active, have clearer goals and motivation.

Worst of all, the voice wasn't working at all, and there was the suggestion that I change the POV from first person to third.

I could have ignored all this advice. Could have just moved on to a third draft in which I didn't change much of anything and instead kept building on what I already had.

Instead I took the mistakes I made to heart, agreed with the points she made, and decided that the only way I was ever going to make this novel better was to *embrace* the mistakes and push myself on the next revision.

In April 2019 I finished changing the POV of the entire novel from first person to third, one of the hardest things I've ever done as a novel writer. I cut five major chapters and two major characters, too, and shortened the novel's timeline from eight days to four days.

I in a sense simplified the novel's story-line while at the same time complicated my main character considerably and added more menace and spookiness to the setting, as well as to the antagonist's backstory.

I'm still working on the manuscript to this day. I'm doing whatever I can to make this manuscript work its best.

But I'm not, in any way, striving for perfectionism.

Perfection might come for a few select genius writers who wrote the right story, at the right time, with the insane amount of talent they carry around with them every day.

But for most of us (i.e., you and me) perfection isn't worth going after.

You know what *is* worth going after, though? Writing the first draft of your novel to the best of your ability, then spending months or years revising it with help from beta readers and people in your world that you trust.

You should be going after ways to make your novel shine even when it's hard, even when you have to cut a quarter of your draft and write new scenes, new characters.

Again, unless you're lucky, you're not going to get it exactly right on that first draft.

Your first draft will not, cannot, be perfect.

What will make you a better writer is coming to terms with your limitations, embracing any flaws you might have in your storytelling, and practicing, practicing, practicing to make it better.

You won't ever get exactly right the first time out. I mean, really, what would be the fun in that? Who wants to read an absolutely perfect novel? What even *is* a perfect novel?

Sometimes the stories that are a little messy are the most compelling. The stories that were written with great passion and a determination to never quit.

Don't obsess over your failures. And don't obsess over what you did wrong if the latest draft of your novel isn't coming together the way you hoped it might.

Just keep moving forward, keep practicing, and write the stories you were born to tell.

28. Why You Need to Avoid Distractions as a Writer

Distractions are everywhere.

In this current day and age, it can be really hard sometimes to find a moment of quiet, a place to think clearly for more than ten seconds.

You have a dozen distractions the minute you wake up in the morning. There's your phone on the night stand. There's the TV remote. There's your stomach growling.

But where distractions *really* come in, maybe more so than in anything else I do throughout the day, is when I'm trying to write my fiction for the day.

I've seen it happen. It can be done. When I know the scene I'm going to write, and I push away all distractions — close the door, turn the phone off, disconnect the Wi-Fi, and so on — I can write 2,000 good words of fiction in about an hour.

There. My work for the entire day. Completed early in the morning. Excellent.

Of course these days are few and far between. Maybe one single day on each manuscript I write.

My typical writing day takes a lot longer. On average, three to four hours. Sometimes five. On rare occasions six or more. There was one day on my MFA thesis novel in the summer of 2017 where I sat down to write 2,000 words at 9am, and I didn't finish those 2,000 words until 7pm. That's right—it took me *ten hours* to write 2,000 words. It was so pathetic I almost cried.

But keep in mind that time passes, and after awhile, when you're deep into revisions, you can never remember which scenes came easier during the drafting process and which ones didn't.

At the end of the day, it doesn't really matter how long it takes you to get your words down on the page, but it will help you, considerably, if you can cut down on the distractions and write your words faster. It's better for your health. It's better for your state of mind. It is better, ultimately, for your novel.

So let's look at the *top three distractions* we all have as fiction writers and figure out how to do away with them during writing time…

1. People

This first distraction may be one of personal preference, but over the years I have tried to write both ways, and I have come to find that writing by yourself, with nobody else around, is the best way to get your words down for the day. You have nobody distracting you, not at a library, or at a coffeehouse, or at a crowded park.

Now, I'll admit, one thing I occasionally like about writing in a public place is that you're sort of forced to focus on your work. When you're at a table at Starbucks, you're not getting up every ten minutes to grab a snack.

But you'll probably have your phone on you, and there's free Wi-Fi, so if you can, try to write at home in a private room by yourself, with the door closed.

2. Phone

This one's huge. I don't know about you, but when I have my phone nearby, I check it constantly. I think most of us do. Five minutes pass, and it's like a tic, I have to look, I have to see if there's a new e-mail, or an alert, or something, anything.

The phone is the kiss of death to fiction writers. The only way to write good words each day is to immerse yourself in the world of your story and put yourself in the heads of your main characters.

When you stop writing every five minutes to check your phone, the spell is broken.

And when you return to your writing, it will take a few minutes, possibly longer, to get back under that spell, and find your groove again.

Reward yourself by messing around on your phone *after* you've written your goal amount of words for the day. Right before you start writing, check it if you need to.

But then take the phone out of the room, put it somewhere far away, and don't retrieve it until you're done writing.

3. Internet

This is the other killer. Oh my God, is it the worst.

Sometimes you click over to the Internet innocently. You can't think of a word. Or want to double check the definition of a word you just used in a sentence.

You look up the word, and read about it, and then, without a moment's hesitation, click on over to Youtube. There's a funny cat video to watch. It's only forty seconds, that's nothing, so you take a look.

Then you watch a second cat video, and a third. No biggie. Three minutes have been lost, who cares.

But then you watch some more videos, and suddenly, in a blink, *two hours* have passed. What a waste.

If there's nothing else you get out of this essay, it's this: Turn. Off. The. Wi-Fi. Before. You. Start. Writing.

And keep it turned off until you reach your words for the day. If you desperately need to look up a definition, put the sentence in bold and then come back to it later!

The Internet is the absolute worst distraction for writers. Because it's so easy to watch some videos, read some articles, scroll through the news feed on Facebook. It's all so pointless, when what really matters is the writing of your fiction. So turn it off.

At the end of the day, there *will* be distractions.

There's family, work, unexpected emergencies. The key is to eliminate as many distractions as possible during the time you choose to get your writing done.

Avoid all distractions… and the rewards will follow.

29. Why You Should Never Compare Yourself to Other Writers

—

Every day you can sit at your writing desk and immediately compare yourself to other authors.

You can compare yourself to people who are more successful than you, and, trust me, it's really easy to do so! People like Stephen King and J.K. Rowling and Angie Thomas and Veronica Roth and countless others.

People who have millions of readers all around the world. People whose novels have been turned into films and television shows. People who are living the dream *you want.*

You can also, of course, compare yourself to people who are less successful than you. People who haven't finished the first draft of a novel yet. People who haven't signed with a literary agent yet. People who sold a book to a traditional publisher, and then it crashed and burned upon release.

The question of course is this: *should* you ever compare yourself to other authors?

The answer, of course, is no.

If you love to write fiction, you should never give up. Giving up is the number one way to fail as a writer. If you give up, it's over. If you keep going, even for one more year, success can absolutely follow.

But the silliness of the question is in the idea that because you may not be as talented or prolific or popular as another author in your genre, then you automatically should stop. If that were the case, hundreds of inspiring, beloved novels wouldn't be on bookshelves today!

If anyone who writes middle grade or young adult fantasy read the first Harry Potter book and then gave up because they could never write anything half as good as J.K. Rowling can, imagine the gluttony of compelling books that would have never been written and published.

My favorite author is Stephen King. Since I was nine years old, I've been writing horror and suspense, and not for one second have I thought I was as good as King.

And you know what? I'm totally fine with that.

I don't try to write like him, and I don't pretend to be him. I take inspiration from his work all the time, particularly his memoir *On Writing*, but if I for one second considered my writing only worthwhile if it was as good as *The Shining* or *It*, I would have given up years ago.

I try to keep other authors out of my mind when I write. It's not healthy to compare your work to someone else's. This extends to not only the writing but also the advances other authors receive, the sales ranks, the fandom.

It's important, of course, to *research* these things, and maybe get an idea about what to expect (and not expect) from the publishing world, but comparing yourself to others, in most every aspect of life, is pointless. And usually hurtful.

It won't make your writing any better, trust me, and will most likely get you to stop writing completely.

Ultimately, the key is to write a lot and read a lot, as Stephen King likes to say.

Read your favorite authors. Read for inspiration. Don't read to emulate and mimic in your own work. Understand the heights that can be reached in a work of prose, and give yourself permission to experiment, but never specifically try to outdo the work of an author you may already immortalize.

Just be you. Write what you love to write, tell the story that you're compelled to tell, and do your best.

Have fun. Try new things. And just keep writing.

30. Don't Let People Make You Feel Bad about Being a Writer

Here's the deal: you will have people in your life who make you feel lousy about being a writer.

And you will also have people who make you feel lousy about writing *in a specific genre.*

Let's start with the first point.

Rarely a month goes by when I don't have someone make me feel lousy about being a writer. Sometimes it's me doubting my own merit, my own worth. Sometimes it's people who suggest that what I do every day isn't a job, isn't a career, it's a *hobby.*

Even after writing twenty novels and graduating with an MFA in Creative Writing, there's *still* that sense that I'm goofing off, not committing to something that's secure.

It's true in some regard that writing has not brought me any financial stability. It brings me stability in a lot of ways, most especially *in my soul,* but nothing I've written has hit in a way yet that would prevent me from having to work a real job.

And you know what? That's okay. It happens to most of us. There's never a guarantee that what you're currently working on will ever go anywhere, or make you a dime, or ever be read.

But when you wake up every morning compelled to write in any way possible, whether it's the whole day if it's available, or just a half-hour you can fit in somewhere in your busy schedule, you need to call yourself a writer. Don't allow people to make you feel lousy about what you do.

And when they do make you feel bad, try if at all possible to distance yourself from that person. You want love in your life. You want support in what you do.

The second point is specific to the kind of content you actually write.

Maybe you only write literary fiction and want to one day win the Pulitzer Prize. Okay, go for it. Maybe you write romance fiction. Or mystery fiction. Or non-fiction. Or erotica. Or poetry.

I believe in two things here. First, write what you want to write. Don't try to write something because you think you *should* be writing it. Instead, write what you love to read, what inspires you, what excites you.

For me it's middle grade and young adult fiction. Since my first year writing novels, I've been pulled toward a few different genres, but I've always loved writing for children. I feel like my voice is best suited to books aimed at younger readers, and it's what I've loved writing the most all these years.

Occasionally I stumble into the world of adult fiction, especially in my short stories, but I'm never as much at home as I am in writing MG and YA fiction.

And the sooner you learn what your niche is, you want to gravitate toward it, write a lot for that niche, fail, fail again, build your knowledge of that niche and keep getting better.

The second thing I believe in is to take that niche you love, whether it's YA or romance or horror or whatever, and *make your writing soar.*

Don't write cheap fiction. Don't think to yourself, well, this is a gruesome horror story so I can write mediocre prose, I can half-ass this. Benjamin Percy has an amazing craft book called *Thrill Me in* which he talks about the importance of merging the high-quality literary fiction with the commercial genre fiction to create books that are *awesome.*

And that's what you want to do, too.

No matter what genre you write in, do your best work, treat it seriously, keep reading, keep writing, keep improving. And don't let anyone deter you from your destiny.

31. Why a Walk Every Day Will Help Your Writing

A little bit of exercise every day is good for your health, first and foremost.

Especially for those of us writers who spend far too many hours every day on our asses in front of a screen, even just thirty minutes of moderate exercise a day can work wonders for your health.

I don't know about you, but on the occasional day I write too much and don't plan well and end up *not* doing any exercise of any kind, I feel almost sick to my stomach. I exercise enough now that when I occasionally skip a day, I feel it, from my head down to my toes. And I don't sleep as well, either.

I wish writing was a more active endeavor, but sadly, it's not, that's just the way it is. So you have to do a little bit of extra work day after day in that you need to find time to write *and* find time to exercise. Both help the other, I think. Exercise clears your mind so you can write better. The act of writing exercises your mind to the point where eventually you need to go outside and work your body instead of your mind.

Something as simple as a short walk is all you really need.

Because you know what else exercise helps with when it comes to your writing? The moment you clear your head and just focus on physical activity, all sorts of ideas might hit you when you least expect it.

I can't tell you how many story problems have worked themselves out in my mind when I go for a walk or a run. When I'm able to step away from the laptop screen and just look at the world around me, not thinking about my story any longer but ideas still coming anyway.

So if you don't exercise as much as you'd like, try to find at least thirty minutes a day to go for a walk.

—

I exercise five to six days a week. Most of these days I either go for an hour run or go to my gym for an hour workout. But sometimes I just want to take a short walk with my dogs, too. As long as I get *some kind* of physical activity in during the day, I feel better health-wise, and my writing improves considerably.

Again, you don't have to do a hard workout. Sometimes a hard workout can make you feel extremely good, and I try for at least two of those a week. But other times a brisk walk will do the trick, too. It depends on what you're comfortable with, and, of course, what you have the time for.

But I guarantee you that even a thirty-minute walk every day will not only help you physically but will also improve your writing, especially when you're at a point in your latest manuscript in which you don't know where to go next or you've hit a story problem you can't seem to fix. Go for a walk, the longer the better.

And maybe by the time you return home, the perfect idea might have fallen right into your lap!

32. Why You Should Listen to Film Scores When You Write

There's a lot that goes into writing a great novel.

Planning, skill, imagination. And, of course, the ability to complete your first draft.

There's no Great American Novel without a finished first draft, and second draft, and third draft, so before you set out to write your masterpiece, you have to figure out how to get your initial words down so you have something to build on, to make into something you feel is worth sending out into the world.

I've already talked about the two ways that will help you reach the end of your first draft. You need to have *consistency* in your writing every day, reaching a chosen word count, and you need to *set a deadline* for your first draft, even it's totally made up.

But what about the very act of getting your words down for the day? Beyond finding a time of the day that works for you, beyond sitting down and knowing for sure the scene you want to work on, what helps get your heart pumping, your imagination soaring?

For me, it's film music.

Since the first day writing my first novel in April 2010, I've been playing film scores through the speakers as I write my fiction. This kind of music always does the job for me because it evokes not an image but a *feeling* I want to express through my words.

It gives me a clear, centered space to do my writing for the day, always letting the other noises around me, and from within my own head, fade away.

Now, these are not songs I'm talking about. I'm not playing Whitney Houston's songs from *The Bodyguard* as I compose my latest novel. I'm not blasting tracks from the latest Marvel movie soundtrack.

The music I listen to while I write new fiction is always wordless scores, with no voices, only melodies that I specifically choose for the kind of work I'm doing.

At the beginning of my writing career, I listened to John Williams.

His iconic scores were always fun to play in the background as I wrote. It wasn't until I wrote my fourth book, however, that I realized that to do better work, I needed to listen to film scores that weren't just great but that actually *added to what I was writing.*

So soon after that I discovered the score to *The Social Network*, composed by Trent Reznor and Atticus Ross.

This score is perfect for many kinds of novels because it drums up feelings of uncertainty, uneasiness, conflict, obsession. It can be anything, really.

What I love about film scores is that, as long as you make the music work in favor of the novel you're trying to put down on the page, then by all means use it! I wrote four novels in 2011 and listened to *The Social Network* as I wrote every one of them.

But then in 2012 I found something even better.

Also by Trent Reznor and Atticus Ross. The score I've written the most novels to, probably ten or more. I recently completed my twentieth novel, and I listened to this score every single day to get my writing done!

It's the score to the 2011 David Fincher film, *The Girl with the Dragon Tattoo.*

I can't tell you how many times I've listened to this music on a long writing day. It is exquisite. Mesmerizing.

And no matter what kind of fiction I'm writing: horror or adventure or quiet literary, this score always seems to do the trick.

It puts me in the right frame of mind. And with this specific score playing through the speakers, I'm never uncertain if I'll hit my 2,000 words for the day. Because I always do.

Whenever I'm stuck in a scene, whenever I'm struggling, I let this music play for a few minutes... and then I'm okay. The score to *The Girl with the Dragon Tattoo* has absolutely been my hidden secret as a writer for all these years. I don't know how much I would've written without it.

I've tried a few different scores, too.

When I wrote my apocalyptic ending to my third *Happy Birthday to Me* book, I spent about a week listening to the ending emotional track The End from *United 93*, which lasts all of six minutes and yet gave me the terrifying mood I needed to make those last couple chapters of *Happy Birthday to You* as emotionally compelling as I could make them.

I've tried writing to some of Hans Zimmer's scores, particularly to the Christopher Nolan movies. His score for *Inception* and *Interstellar* are incredible, and of course his work on the *Dark Knight* trilogy is superb. My problem with some of this work is that it's almost too overwhelming in its grandiosity, and sometimes makes me lose my way.

The truth is nothing has gotten as many words out of me as fast as the score to *The Girl with the Dragon Tattoo*.

I don't really have an answer for why. It's just great, great writing music. And always will be.

So I don't really know how you do it. Maybe you prefer silence, which *just doesn't* work for me. Maybe you prefer lots of voices surrounding you, like in coffeehouses or on a college campus. This works better for me than silence, but still, it's not ideal. Maybe you like listening to actual songs instead of score, or classical music. Whatever works for you, keep at it.

But if you've never written a first draft of a novel before, if you're intimidated by the idea of it but still very much want to do it, listening to film scores is a tool I absolutely believe will help you.

Again, it's not about shaping your story in any concrete way. It's about instilling a feeling inside yourself that will keep you focused on your writing and keep you on track to reach your goal word count for the day.

Give this practice a try. You may be surprised at how much, and how *well*, you write in the future!

33. Why You Need to Use the Best Vocabulary You Have as a Writer

This may be one of the hardest things to learn as a writer.

You do not, under any circumstance, need to *stretch your vocabulary* to make it as an author. You don't need to go through your second or third draft and "dress up" your vocabulary, changing the occasional word in a sentence with something more colorful you discovered in the thesaurus.

Yes, there are successful authors with amazing vocabularies. The one I always go to is Donna Tartt and *The Goldfinch*. I read all 800 pages of that book in complete awe of her mastery of vocabulary and language. In any given paragraph I was amazed by what I was seeing.

And I also recognized that if I lived to be 1000 years old, I could never do what she does.

I don't have an impressive vocabulary in my writing. Sometimes I'll surprise myself with an amazing sentence that I go back and read later and pat myself on the back. When you're in the zone, when you're *so connected* to your story and characters that real life effectively falls into the background, you can write some truly incredible things, that's for sure.

Sometimes these fabulous sentences stay in the manuscript. Other times they go. I can't tell you how much great writing, some of my best really, has had to be deleted in the long run.

Here's the deal, ultimately: no matter how amazing your vocabulary is, if the scene doesn't help the story and characters, it needs to go.

You cannot, under any circumstances, keep a scene in your novel that shouldn't be there just because the vocabulary is well-chosen, just because the scene reads beautifully.

One of the hardest things to do is delete good writing. Writing that might make someone smile, that might make a professor of English somewhere say, *damn, this writer's good.*

But you know what's one of the easiest things for me to do? Something that took me only a few books to master?

Write the first draft of the novel—and all the other drafts too, really—with the vocabulary I already have.

I'll be honest that yes, sometimes I do use the dictionary and thesaurus.

Usually it's for help when I can't find the right word to describe something, but always these tools are last resorts.

You should at the end of the day pick the word that feels right and then keep going. If that word really, really bugs you three drafts down the road, you can always take a minute and try to change it to something else.

But please don't fret about the strength of your vocabulary, or lack thereof. The reader is not going to care if your vocabulary isn't spectacular.

Your reader is going to care about a *great story well told*, so get to doing that first and foremost!

34. Why You Need to Use the First Word that Comes to Mind When You Write

When you're writing your fiction, you make hundreds and hundreds of word choices every day, oftentimes without realizing it.

And that's how you should be putting your first draft on the page. Without overthinking things, especially when it comes to the words you choose to put in any given scene.

Revisions down the road come in small shapes and big shapes. Sometimes you have to cut long chapters. Other times you have to re-write a sentence and give it a better word at the end. Yes, there will be times in revision when you have to start looking at specific words that may need changing.

But when you're writing the first draft of your novel, you should always, always, always *pick the first word that comes to mind.*

Do not, under any circumstances, stop the process of writing to look up a word in the dictionary or thesaurus.

If you're *really* stuck on what the best word should be in the sentence, write the best one that comes to mind, and move on.

Trust me on this.

When you come back to that sentence six weeks or three months or a year from now, whenever you begin the revising process, most likely a better word will enter your mind when you re-read the sentence.

This happens to me often. I will get stuck in the first draft on a single word, but when I come back to that sentence months later, a much better one comes to mind. And that's without looking in a dictionary.

Another reason not to hang up on a given word is tied to what I said before—odds are you will be cutting that word, and sentence, in later revisions.

One last reason not to panic about your word choice?

Often the first word you come up with… *is the best one!* You can sit there for twenty minutes trying to think of something better, but more often than not, the first word you put down is actually the best of all, and you don't need to go searching for anything else.

Once you're in the thick of revisions, and especially when the book is shining its brightest and in you're in the glorious stage of copy-editing, then yes, do pay attention to your word choices.

As you slowly read through your sentences, do change a word here and there if you think a better one would be suited.

But the process of the first draft is different. The first draft is about *getting your story down on paper*, nothing else.

Use the first word that comes to mind and move onto the next sentence.

35. Why Grammar Needs to be at the Top of Your Toolbox

Grammar is an element of writing everyone struggles with, that's for damn sure.

I like to think of myself as pretty adept at the grammar side of things, and teaching freshman composition for the past seven years has certainly helped with that considerably.

I also had amazing high school English teachers who drilled the fundamentals of grammar into me like you wouldn't believe. I definitely came out of tenth grade feeling like I'd just been through an advanced college course in everything grammar!

And yet I still make mistakes, trust me. I have people all the time tell me I use commas too often. I have people make the kinds of corrections to my sentences that make me hang my head in shame.

The simple truth is that we are all going to make mistakes in grammar.

First drafts are especially messy when it comes to things like grammar. Because you're going to be revising your manuscript considerably, the grammar in the first draft doesn't have to be perfect.

You can have typos all over the place. You can write so fast that when you look back over your work weeks later you might not have a clue what the occasional sentence even means.

As I've discussed before, what you want to do in your first draft is *get your story down*. Don't panic about vocabulary, grammar, things like that.

At the same time, you are not, under any circumstances, allowed to turn away from the rules of grammar, write sentences and paragraphs however you like, and then expect your beta readers or your literary agent or your editor to fix what you consider "minor issues."

Grammar is minor, sure, especially in the large scope of your novel, but when your beta reader or workshop classmate can't get through the first page of your manuscript because it's riddled with errors, there's a huge problem.

At the end of the day, you need to take grammar seriously.

I've participated in about ten creative writing workshops in my life, workshops meant for serious writers with serious talent, and it always baffled me and frustrated me when a student submitted a workshop story that had a hundred typos, and a grammatical error in practically every sentence.

Nobody will *ever* take you seriously if you don't take your grammar seriously.

It's one thing to make mistakes in the first draft and then fix them to the best of your ability later. It's another to just brush off grammar as that annoying outlier that doesn't concern you.

So if you struggle with grammar, do your homework. Read some craft books. Write a lot. Revise a lot. As is the case with anything, *you will get better*.

And as long as you take the grammar element of writing seriously, you'll be just fine in the long run.

36. Why Fragments are So Important in Your Writing

The poor fragment. Why is it hated so?

Throughout high school I was taught to never use a fragment. That every sentence I wrote had to be a complete sentence. That my work would be marked down if I included even one lone fragment.

The truth is each genre of writing comes with its own set of rules and expectations. The reason we learn in high school never to use fragments is that, for the most part, *academic* writing shouldn't have fragments.

I would argue that the occasional fragment is acceptable if you're relating a personal story or allowed to give the piece a little of your own voice. But if the piece is meant for a job application, or for a strict professor who has no sense of humor, then yes, you would be best served to write in only complete sentences.

For the longest time, I struggled to allow myself to write fragments. Even in my novels.

Fragments would look awkward on the page, and in revisions I would often cut the fragment completely or alter the sentence slightly to make it a complete sentence. I was taught for so long to not write fragments, so why put them in my work now?

The answer is simply this: *rhythm.*

It's not something that can really be learned or taught. It's not something that comes easily to every writer. It's certainly something you can study through reading lots and lots of books, in a variety of genres.

And it's something you'll learn not necessarily in the writing of your first novel, but in the third or the fourth.

The rhythm of your sentences, especially in a long work of fiction, is incredibly important. How much description you include, how much dialogue, how many big paragraphs mixed in with shorter paragraphs—all vital.

But the rhythm of the sentences themselves also make a huge impact on whomever is reading your book. No matter what genre of fiction you work in, writing one complete sentence after another for pages on end might look grammatically correct to *you*, the writer, but it won't provide the best possible experience for the reader.

You want the sentences to find such a glorious rhythm that the reader can't stop flipping through the pages, simple as that.

And keep in mind, too: most readers won't read every sentence. I can't tell you how often I randomly skim a paragraph or a page, even in a book I'm loving. I'm sure there are some readers who savor every word of a novel, but I would assume most at least occasionally skim.

And you know when they will skim most often?

When you have big block paragraphs with only long, complete sentences, and no fragments.

When the language becomes intimidating, lengthy, verbose, you might lose a few of your readers.

And even in longer paragraphs, fragments can help with this problem.

So please—*don't be afraid of fragments.*

I wouldn't overload your prose with them by any means. Have no fragments, and your writing can become stale and arduous. Have too many fragments, and your writing looks downright silly.

It's important to find the right balance, but you absolutely want the fragment to be your friend.

Experiment with them. Try a couple of them in a page of your writing. Put a fragment in the middle of a paragraph in between two longer sentences.

Remember to think about *rhythm* in your writing, and the more experience you get, the better this rhythm will become.

Yes, even with the occasional fragment!

37. Why Beginnings and Endings are So Important in Your Writing

Beginnings and endings are so important in your storytelling. Mess up the beginning and the reader might not continue on. Mess up the ending and the reader might forget all the wonderful things that came before and instead put your story down unsatisfied.

Let's look at Beginnings first…

1. You have ten pages to grab the attention of your reader.

The writer's job is to keep the reader turning pages. The first ten pages are absolutely the most crucial because the reader will often stop if they're not impressed.

Others might suggest you have even *less* than ten pages to grab a reader. Some might suggest you have one or two pages, and that's definitely the case with some people.

Make sure you hook that reader in… and then don't let them go!

2. The beginning of your story can be active and exciting, but it doesn't have to be.

It can be more expository or slower-paced, that's totally fine. But there should be something that *intrigues* your reader quickly.

The story you are telling dictates, in a sense, the opening you choose. Genre, for example, also plays a huge part.

Don't start your story on a car chase because you think that's what will get readers excited to read on. Make sure your opening makes sense with the kind of story you're writing.

3. The reader should know in the first ten pages what the story is about and whom it's about.

Think of the first ten pages of your story as its own unit, its own block of dramatic action. It must be executed with efficiency and dramatic value because it sets up everything that follows.

And if by the end of ten pages, you reader doesn't have a clue what your story is about or whom it's about? That's a major problem.

It's why prologues are often looked down upon. It's why agents always request the first ten pages—they want to see what your story's about, and whom it's about, and how strong of a writer you are.

Wow your readers in the beginning, and you're well on your way!

OK, now let's look at Endings in your writing…

1. You must know your ending before you begin writing.

You don't have to know it *exactly*. It doesn't have to be totally fully-formed in your mind.

But you should have a clear idea of where your story is going at all times. An endpoint that feels right to you. I never begin a new short story or a novel without at least *some idea* of what the final scene will be, some idea of what happens to my protagonist by the end of the narrative.

If you have no idea where your story is headed, you will get lost at some point, I guarantee you.

2. You don't have to know every specific detail about the ending, though, and feel free to change the ending later.

Your ending can change a little as you begin the drafting process, and it can change a lot as you go about your chapters.

And you know what? You can completely change the ending later if you feel like the progression of the plot ultimately has pulled your characters in a different direction, that's okay.

But you need to start with something. Billy Wilder once said, *if you have a problem with your ending, the answer lies in the beginning.* To write a strong opening... you simply need to know your ending.

3. Here's the truth of the matter: beginnings are difficult, and endings are really, really difficult!

Endings are so hard to get right because they have to be satisfying for the reader, make an emotional impact, not be contrived or predictable, not be forced or fabricated, and resolve all the main story points in a way that makes sense.

It has to work. Or everything that came before might have been for nothing.

Don't end your story with the main character committing suicide. Don't end it with everybody dying in a shoot-out.

Think of something original, something unexpected. Think of something that will leave your reader grinning from ear to ear when they put down your book.

There's so much that goes into great storytelling, so many things you need to think about.

But beginnings and endings should absolutely be at the forefront of your mind as you draft and revise!

38. Here are 5 Terrible Ways to Start Your Novel

One of the trickiest elements of writing a novel is starting your story where you're supposed to.

Starting in the right place, starting in the most dynamic place, hooking in your reader on that opening page in a way that feels dramatic, earned, and not gimmicky.

You work on a novel for months and months, sometimes years. You put *so much work* into every chapter, every paragraph, every sentence.

But the sad truth of the matter is that nothing really matters more than that opening page. I know you don't want to hear this—I don't even like thinking it—but all that hard work might be for nothing in the long run *if you have a shitty first page.*

If the book really takes off in Chapter 2 and remains a glorious ride all the way to the end, that probably won't matter because 90% of your potential readers might bail in the less successful Chapter 1.

There are a gazillion books out there. And there are a gazillion reasons for a reader to not pick up your book. So there's really no excuse to write a bad opening page to your novel.

Now, keep in mind, you don't have to get it exactly right in your first draft. Or even in your second or your third. You'll tweak your opening page over and over. You might rewrite it once or twice down the road.

Even when your novel is completely done and you can't look at it one more time, you will still occasionally comb through that opening page like no other page in the manuscript.

At a very basic level, what are some things you should very much avoid doing in the opening page of your novel? Here are *five*…

1. Open with a huge block paragraph of description.

This is the number one no-no. When I see a huge block paragraph of description on page one, I'll probably start reading and give the opening chapter a chance… but I also might not.

Block paragraphs are hard on the eyes, and the agents and editors who pick up your novel likely won't want to see them so early in your manuscript before they've become invested in the characters and story.

Feel free to open with a fully formed paragraph, fine. Your novel doesn't need to open with one-sentence paragraphs to entice your reader to read further.

But you should definitely think about how long is too long when it comes to the paragraphs on your first page. Is something urgent happening in them?

Or are the paragraphs all about description? Description of the setting, description of your protagonist. You have so much time to integrate description. Don't do it in the first paragraph unless you have a very good reason to.

Be wary of description in your opening pages unless that description very much adds something crucial!

2. Open with your main character waking up.

This one is probably the most obvious, but I have actually done it before. I've accidentally started a novel not just once but *twice* with my protagonist waking up in the morning, and it wasn't until the revision process where I realized the horrible mistake I had made.

Opening your novel with your character waking up is most often a cliché. Especially if it's a boring moment of your character waking up in the morning after a good night's sleep, you're definitely in trouble. You want to open your novel on a unique image, a compelling moment that draws your reader into the conflict and world of your characters.

Don't ruin what might otherwise be a great novel by opening with a cliché like this one.

It might seem like the easy way into your story, but almost 100% of the time, it's just an excuse to shoot yourself in the foot long before you're even started writing Chapter 2.

3. Open in the middle of an action scene.

Now this one can work in specific circumstances, but you really have to be careful with it.

I tried doing this on a recent young adult thriller, and I thought it worked great, a big hook happening in the opening sentence that drew you into an extremely intense car chase that lasted the first seven pages of the novel.

After having that opening chapter workshopped by writing colleagues, I soon realized that opening in a scary action scene didn't ultimately work because my readers *didn't yet care about the characters.*

My characters didn't get a real introduction of any kind until Chapter 2, and that element annoyed not just some but *all* of my readers. They recognized what I was trying to do by starting right with the action, but everyone suggested opening on a quieter moment before the mayhem would be a better way to go.

Now the car chase begins in Chapter 4 of the novel, and the first three chapters deal with the characters first. And upon re-reading the book recently, I realized how crucial it was to make you care about the two main characters before the action begins.

You can certainly experiment opening with action in your novel. You certainly want to start with conflict as early as possible.

Just keep in mind that if the reader doesn't yet care about your protagonist, you might be better served to open on a quieter moment, not halfway through a chase scene.

4. Open with lots of dialogue.

This is kind of similar to opening with action because in some regard you think you're hooking the reader in by using dialogue. It might be colorful dialogue, striking dialogue. It might be back-and-forth banter that makes you laugh out loud! Or grit your teeth in anticipation!

But here's the problem with having dialogue be the first thing your readers see—they don't know who the characters are yet. Just like with action, opening with dialogue is tricky because the reader's not going to be invested in the conversation due to a lack of investment in any characters.

I think one line of dialogue, followed immediately by action, can potentially be a solid way to start a novel. One line of dialogue that strikes a mood, or that shows off the voice of your main character, and then going right into a few short paragraphs of conflict and tension that reveals who your protagonist is. That might work great, actually.

But when a reader is thrown into the middle of a long conversation, two or more people talking back and forth where there's not a clue indication of who's talking or who these characters even are, you're in trouble.

5. Open with a dream.

Again, the ultimate cliché. Again, a huge no-no.

And this one is the worst because you might draw your reader into your novel for a page or two or three, and then as soon as you reveal that opening tension was just your protagonist's dream, you will likely alienate 95% or more of your readers.

Even worse, once the reader is annoyed by discovering those awesome opening pages were a dream, then the reader is annoyed a second time by reading about your protagonist waking up in bed from that dream and going about their morning!

So in effect you're making two fatal mistakes here— opening with a dream *and* opening with your main character waking up.

Avoid, avoid, avoid!

These are just a few of the terrible ways to start your novel.

I'm sure agents and editors could give you fifty more. Like not starting with a conflict. Like starting with a prologue. Like starting with too much world building. Like starting with too many characters. Like starting with too much backstory.

Finding the right way and right place to start your novel comes with lots and lots of practice as a writer. You write enough fiction and you read enough books and watch enough movies and you start to understand the kinds of opening that work well, and that don't work at all.

Just keep in the back of your mind that the opening five pages, and yes, even the very first page, are crucial to the success of your novel, there's no way around it.

So take some extra time to think about how you're going to start your story. You'll be much better off in the long run!

39. Why You Need to be Careful about Prologues in Your Writing

Here's something I should get off my chest right away: I actually *love* a good prologue.

Yes, even when they're not entirely necessary. There's something about slowly discovering the tone of a book, the mood of it, the *world* of it, especially if we're reading a story not set completely in our current reality. Prologues have the ability to transport us to a new place without necessarily dropping us right into the action or the conflict of the main character.

I read often. I'm trying to read one new novel a week, but lately that's been more like one novel every two weeks. And let me tell you, I see prologues *all the time.*

I'd say I see them in one in every four novels I read. And often I like what the prologue does. I like how by the first sentence of chapter one I have a clear understanding of what kind of book I'm getting myself into.

However, it's not always the best idea to have a prologue.

I believe at the end of the day it depends on the story you're trying to tell. And I also believe at the end of the day that many, many agents and editors out there might not take so kindly to you including a prologue in your novel.

There's definitely a rationale to this. Lots of books are published every week, and lots of readers pick up a book and want to be hooked from that very first page. And there is the sense that if a reader picks up a book and sees a prologue first, one that has little to do with the main story or protagonist, that reader might put the book down and move onto the next.

If you feel like your book doesn't need a prologue, and that you would be best suited to start on a scene with your protagonist, *do it.* If you're not sure what to do, avoid the prologue. Don't include a prologue unless you have a really, really good idea about what to do with it and that you feel your story wouldn't be as powerful without it.

Unless you're self-publishing your novel, you're likely going to have to make the case for your prologue to your agent, to your editor.

So yes, be very thoughtful when it comes to including a prologue in your latest novel.

If you don't feel the novel needs a prologue, then don't pursue it, but if you feel really strongly that you need one, feel free to write it, and keep in mind you might have to cut it later for various reasons.

When it comes to the prologue, you really do need to make it awesome. If that's the first thing your reader is going to see, make sure it's incredible!

Use it as more than a way to hook the reader. Don't let it make up for the fact that chapters one through five are super boring.

Openings are critical to your success as a novel writer. You can write the best book of all time, but if your first ten pages suck, you're in trouble. It's one of the great injustices in fiction writing, but it's the way it is. If your opening doesn't work, few readers will continue on. Including a prologue is another way to screw up the beginning of your novel, so only include one if you feel like it *has to be there.*

But, one more time, prologues can absolutely make a novel better when done right. I still see them all the time, and I've even tried doing a few of them myself. So go for it if you want. Try something unique and out of the box if you feel compelled to.

Just keep in mind that prologues aren't for everybody, and that you need to be careful.

Prologue or no problem, make sure the opening of your novel is as great as it can be!

40. Why the Situation of Your Story is So Important

It's intimidating to write a novel.

There's so much work ahead. So much joy, and frustration, and laughter, and sadness. Months and probably years of work are ahead of you.

Yes, *it's going to be hard.*

There's a novel I wrote at the end of 2015, and I didn't complete the final draft of it until early 2019. The book went through *seventeen drafts* over three and a half years. It was the kind of long haul of revision I never could have imagined, but you know what's one of the major elements that got me through it?

The situation of the book was and still is so damn compelling to me.

The idea of a twelve-year-old aspiring movie director who wants to make the best monster movie ever… by going in search of *real monsters?* It was one of those ideas that popped into my head one day and made me smile, and I just knew I had to write it. Especially since I had experience making movies as a kid, I thought there was something fun I could bring to that manuscript.

When I started, I didn't have all the characters fleshed out yet. I didn't have the setting, or the time of year, or even what kind of monsters I wanted to feature.

I didn't even know the middle and end of the novel either.

But I had the situation—and it was a good one.

I had the "What-If" question Stephen King talks a lot about. If your situation can be expressed through a one-sentence What-If question, you're already halfway there. If your situation is too complicated or maybe not complicated enough to be expressed in a What-If question, you might be in trouble.

If you can come up with a really strong "What If" question, that might be *all you need* to get you motivated to write your book for weeks and months to come.

Some people suggest you should start with your main character, their need and goal, and what is keeping them from that goal. Yes, this is *extremely important.* Yes, you should come up with this early on.

But I disagree that this is necessarily what you should start with.

The *first* thing you should come up with is the situation of your story. Not the genre, or the main character. What kind of *situation* is happening? What's the unique premise of your book that is going to compel people to want to read it?

Think of five books you love. Then think of five films you love. Take all ten and try to whittle their stories down into a one-sentence "What-If" question. You'll probably find it's easy to do!

You want your own "What-If" question to be easy, too.

And it should get you excited to get started.

Books are written in all kinds of different ways. There are so many different stages and methods.

But always, always, always start with a strong situation. You'll be glad you did!

41. Why Dynamic Characters are So Important in Your Fiction Writing

Yes, the situation of your story is important.

It's essential. Without a compelling situation, no reader is going to want to read it. Or possibly even pick up your story in the first place.

But coming up with your situation is only the first step. The next part you need to think long and hard about? Your characters, of course!

You can write the world's most thrilling, entertaining, surprising, riveting adventure novel, but if the characters are weak and flat on the page, if they speak in ways that are awkward, if there's nothing motivating them and making them go after a specific goal, your reader *won't care.*

Let me repeat that. Without dynamic, three-dimensional characters in your story, your reader will not care!

Once you've come up with a great situation, now it's time to sit down and flesh out your characters.

Start with your protagonist.

Who is the lead of your story? What's the gender? What's the age? Where do they live? What do they look like? What is their backstory? What are they actively going after? What's the goal?

Figuring out your protagonist is the first important part to coming up with your cast of characters. Don't begin by thinking about the supporting character. Focus on the *main* character, and don't move on to anyone else until you have a strong grip on that character.

This is a stage of your writing you can't rush, and you can't skip. Don't think to yourself, okay, my protagonist is a thirty-year-old woman looking for love. She lives in Pittsburgh, and she's five-foot-three, and she's got long blond hair.

Nope, sorry, that's not enough.

You can't just think of five or six key details and then jump right into your story. You need to be *super clear* about your protagonist in every way, not just in their physical appearance, but in their life story, body language, method of speaking, voice, everything.

Even things that will never show up on the page. Things in their past that might inform the character but doesn't actually play itself out in the plot.

Doesn't matter. *You* need to know it.

And you need to have a fully-realized character before you move on to the next step.

Open a blank Word document page and write a character bio. Write down as much about the character as you can think of. Free-write if you want for ten minutes straight. Write until you can't think of anything else!

Write enough about your protagonist so that you have a solid handle on what makes them tick.

Only then should you move on to your supporting characters.

Take the five most important ones and write a detailed character bio for each, not quite as detailed as the bio for your protagonist, but detailed nonetheless.

Write down physical traits, interior traits, backstory, character goals, and the like. Fill up pages and pages just talking about your characters.

You can use this later when you get stuck in a scene and maybe don't know how the character would react to a piece of surprising news. Or what words that character might say in this particular exchange of dialogue.

Once you have some pages written on your supporting characters, now move on to the more minor characters. Ones who appear in your book but aren't quite as important as the main few.

These bios can be shorter. Like four or five sentences. Give a few physical details, maybe something about what they're going after or trying to find or whatever it is, then move on to the next character.

Once you have written down all the characters you can think of, it's time to close the document for a day or two, then go back and read through everything you've written.

Change what you want to change. Keep the same what you want to keep the same.

Once you feel good about your character bios and are confident you have a strong handle on at least your major characters, particularly the protagonist, it's time to move on to the next stage.

Now it's time to write your story.

No matter what, do not start your next writing project until you have outlined and written about and thought deeply about your characters!

It's pivotal that you not write one-dimensional characters that have nothing to say and nothing to do.

Characters that are mere clichés of people we've seen in a hundred other stories.

Make your characters unique, original, fascinating, groundbreaking. Do something new. Create relationships that are unusual. Write about someone most people have never read about before.

Do what you can to make for characters that excite the reader and make them want to read on even if they're not intensely engaged in the plot.

Find a compelling situation for your story, and come up with dynamic, three-dimensional characters that ring true, and you will be well on your way to writing a fantastic novel!

42. Why the Protagonist of Your Novel Should Have an Interesting Profession

What is it that's so fascinating in reading about someone's job in a novel?

I don't know about you, but when the protagonist has a profession that plays a large role in the story, I get excited. I'm curious about what they do for a living.

And I want to see that profession developed on the page, not just tossed aside like a quick description.

We're all interested in what people do to make money. In what people do for forty hours or more a week to earn a living and put food on the table.

But for the most part we never get an inside look into what other people do for jobs. We hear stories from friends, we see news reports on TV, we visit the doctor and the dentist of course, but rarely do we get *up close and personal* with someone's occupation.

That's what's so great about fiction.

Whether the book is written in first person or third, if the author takes an interest in the lead character's profession and doesn't push it aside in order to get to the plot, then the reader often gets an intimate look at the person's job, and all those details, at least to me, are fascinating.

Most of my novels have been written for the young adult market, so the jobs for my characters are pretty much school, sports, extracurricular activities, homework. You know... things sixteen-year-olds do.

The parents in my stories always have jobs, yes, but I often don't give a glimpse into their occupations because the focus of the narrative is always on their son or daughter.

But showing people's work is something I can do more of in the future. And you know what? So should you!

When an author puts a lot of effort into research, and then develops not just a flawed, three-dimensional, super interesting character but also that character's *work life*, a job that one might not know anything about, I'm delighted in the details, in the scenes that show what they are passionate in doing on a daily basis. You get to be told a great story but also learn something new you didn't know before.

Again, this is why fiction is so amazing. Non-fiction too, of course. And so many films and television shows. To get a glimpse into someone's occupation, how it works, why it's important, what it means to that character, is a truly special part of storytelling.

And when that job comes alive on the page in a way that's authentic and true, it's always a total thrill for the reader!

43. Why Good Description Makes for the Best Writing

I'm going to confess something: after years of practice, I'm *still* not great at description.

There's a lot I do well. I can whip up compelling story-lines and relatable main characters. I'm pretty good at pacing and dialogue. And I adore chapter cliffhangers.

But the one area I've always struggled a bit is description. It's a facet of writing I've tried to get better at over the years but that I still don't take enough time to master.

Because it's not just about how to write the description. You can't just go through your manuscript and add description here and there to the settings, to your character's physical traits, and then be done with it.

It's a matter of *how much to.*

Some places in your novel will need more description than others. Some characters will need to be described in detail, and for other characters, you might only need a few well-chosen words.

A setting that's integral to your story-line might need a few sentences of specific description that gives the reader a crystal-clear image, and other settings might not need any description at all.

Ultimately the description needs to flow in a way that it never actually *reads* like description.

If you stop your story from chugging along by adding a paragraph of description, you might lose the reader. You might destroy the magic of the story!

Even if that description is extremely well-written. Even if that description oozes fantastic imagery.

If the description slows your story down, you need to either trim it or toss it.

Some of your readers will want more story and less description. Others might love to read description and want lots more of it. The trick is to find the best middle ground possible.

Enough description to appease readers, but not so much that you drag down your readers.

So what happens when you have little to no description of any settings or characters?

The reader becomes confused. It can be hard to place who everybody is, where the characters are located in one scene to the next. It's not enough to just say that one of your supporting characters has blond hair, and that a scene takes place in a large neighborhood park. You need to give the reader more than that.

But, again, don't stop the narrative cold to deliver a paragraph of description of the girl or of the park.

Good description is a learned skill because throughout many years and manuscripts you learn how to sprinkle description into your work in tiny doses, never in large doses or all at once.

Instead of describing the blond girl when the protagonist first meets her, have a sentence or two of description up front, then give us some description later in her first scene, maybe after a line of dialogue, and then add a bit of description five chapters later, when the girl is in another scene.

Don't give us *everything* we need to know description-wise right away. It can be overwhelming.

Save some things for later. Give the reader enough description so that the person or setting makes sense, and that an image can be rendered the reader's mind, but not so much to stop the story.

Because what happens when you have too much description?

The reader gets bored. Aggravated. *Annoyed.*

I know I do. It's why I've had difficulty reading classic novels over the years, because when the author stops to describe a hat for a page-long paragraph, I immediately check out.

I really, really struggle when it comes to big paragraphs of description. At the end of the day, I just don't care.

Tell me enough to give me an image, then move the story along. I'm always more interested in the conflict, the rising of the stakes, than I am in your five gorgeous sentences describing what the lake looks like under a full moon.

Practice is key when it comes to writing, and it's especially key when you're writing description.

Trust me, I *still* struggle with it sometimes, although I've definitely gotten better at it. I've learned how to sprinkle description here and there that give the reader an image but that doesn't go on and on for an entire paragraph.

This is why, as always, it's important to read a lot and write a lot. Keep writing, and keep learning, and you'll get there.

44. Why Dialogue is So Important in Defining Your Characters

I've learned a lot about writing fiction since I penned my first novel in 2010, but one of the most important things I've learned by far is the necessity for dialogue that helps define your characters.

Dialogue is used for all sorts of reasons in fiction. It helps with pacing. It offers white space on the page, which is typically pleasing for the reader. It helps further along your narrative. It gives the reader information. It breaks up exposition with specific scenes.

Without dialogue, a novel might never fully come to life. I've read a lot of books over the years where an author uses dialogue sparingly, where ten pages or more go by and all you're reading are big block paragraphs of exposition.

Sometimes this works if the story is so ridiculously compelling that the exposition is enough. And sometimes this works if the main character is alone for long stretches of time.

But for the most part, *you're going to need dialogue*, probably in every scene if not every chapter, and you want to use it in ways that fit those five criteria above.

But another way dialogue is useful? Essential, even?

Dialogue helps define your characters.

I've always been decent at dialogue in my fiction writing. I'm good at finding a rhythm to the dialogue in the scene and making it long enough to convey the necessary information but short enough that the reader doesn't feel like I'm delivering the *entire* conversation between two people—the beginning, middle, and end.

You typically don't want that in a dialogue scene. You want to write the part that is necessary for the reader.

So yeah, dialogue is my jam. I love reading it. I love writing it. Most of my novels have lots and lots of dialogue.

But the one area in dialogue I've always struggled a bit is in using it to define my characters. Not because I don't want it to, but because it's often *so damn difficult.*

Before you begin any fiction writing project, you want to define your major characters in other ways, like physical attributes, backstories, motivations. These are all key to understand before you get started.

But one other way you should be thinking about your characters is in what they say, and how they say it.

Bottom line is this: if every character in your book talks in exactly the same way, you're in trouble.

If the protagonist and the best friend and the girlfriend and the antagonist all speak in a similar way, a similar rhythm, with similar words, etc, you're not working hard enough.

It might even be worth doing a revision where you focus solely on the dialogue and how it defines each of your characters. Not just the main character. But pretty much anyone who speaks at one point or another in the manuscript.

One method that helps with this? Reading your dialogue *out loud*.

I typically don't read the prose of my novels out loud, but at some point during the revising process, I read my dialogue out loud to get a sense of voice and language.

I don't want my protagonist to speak one way in Chapter 2 and then another way in Chapter 20 if there's not a good reason. I want to make sure the voices of my characters stay consistent.

Another method that's been suggested to me is looking at each scene of your story from the point-of-view of every character that exists in that scene.

So even if your book is written in the first person of your main character, you should still read through the scene once trying to see the world through the eyes of the *second* character that appears in the scene, and the third and the fourth, depending on how many characters show up.

Does the dialogue feel authentic? Is the dialogue defining the characters, as well as their wants and needs?

You're not going to get all the dialogue right on the first draft. The first draft is going to be messy, and all that's important about it, really, is *finishing it*. Getting a draft of your novel finished means now you can truly start writing it because you have a base to work from. Now you can see what dialogue of yours is working, and what needs cutting or adding. Maybe you'll have to write a completely new version.

Dialogue serves so many purposes. And there needs to be a reason why each line of dialogue is there in your story. If a short exchange between two characters adds nothing to your story? Delete it.

And if the dialogue isn't help defining your characters well enough? Keep working and keep revising.

45. Why the Best Form of Dialogue Attribution is 'Said'

The earlier you learn this rule the better.

I genuinely believe there's little lenience here, even though, I know, you might get bored using "said" all the time. You might want to punch up your writing a bit with other options.

Maybe instead of having Charlie *say* a line of dialogue, you want him to cry it! Or wail it! Or implore it! Maybe you want him to *quietly sigh it*.

What you will find and hopefully learn fast when you start writing a lot is that when you pen a scene of heavy dialogue, the creativity of your work comes through in everything that *surrounds* your dialogue attribution. In the dialogue itself. In a sentence that precedes or follows the attribution.

It should *not* come in the dialogue attribution itself, remember that.

Here's the deal with dialogue attributions: you want them to be practically invisible to your readers. The reader should fixate on everything surrounding it, but not the "John said" part.

The "John said" is there for one reason only: to highlight what character is talking in this particular line. That's what I use dialogue attribution for, always. To make sure the reader knows exactly who is speaking and when.

Lots of dialogue attribution is a matter of how many characters are in a scene. If you have a long dialogue scene between two people, you might not have to use dialogue attributions as much.

You have Thelma and Kevin talking at a bar, you don't need to have "Thelma said" on one line and "Kevin said" on the next.

After awhile, trust that your reader knows who is saying what, and if your characters' voices are coming through, you can keep the dialogue attributions to a minimum.

But what if you have three or more characters in a scene? This is where it gets tricky.

If you have three or more characters, you will need dialogue attributions often.

Unless there's a specific moment where two of the characters are bantering back and forth in the midst of the larger conversation, keep those dialogue attributions handy.

At the same time, you do want to mix things up a little. You don't want twenty lines of new dialogue in a row with "Adam said" and "Leslie said" and "Brandon said" and so on. It gets monotonous.

But this doesn't mean you need to substitute "said" for some fancier word. You almost never *want* to substitute "said."

If you want to use something besides "said," try these…

1. Ask.

This is the most common one outside of "said." If a character is asking a question, I almost always use "ask" instead of "said."

I have seen the word "said" in dialogue attributions following a character asking a question, but I'm on the side of using "ask" whenever possible. This one you can use as much as you want.

2. Whisper.

I have characters whisper lines of dialogue occasionally, and when I do so, it's always for a good reason.

Don't just use "whisper" to mix things up. Use "whisper" when there's a deliberate reason the dialogue needs to be quieter. Use this dialogue attribution to a minimum, just a few specific times in a manuscript.

3. Shout.

You might find other authors who believe in still using "said" even when the character is shouting a line of dialogue across the room, but I always think that looks weird on the page.

I write a lot of horror and suspense, and so there are typically moments where characters are screaming and shouting dialogue, and so occasionally I'll put "Mike shouted" after a line of dialogue that's meant to be extremely loud. Like with "whisper," keep these to a minimum but the occasional use I think is okay.

I've also very rarely had a character "scream" a line of dialogue, and that is only when I've had a long scene of dialogue of characters constantly shouting to the point that I want to avoid using "shout" one more time.

That's about it. I'd guess ninety percent of my dialogue attributions is "said," eight percent or so is "ask," and two percent is for these other uses.

Again, "said" is always your best choice. It's invisible on the page. It's just there to tell the reader who is talking.

Dialogue attribution provides rhythm, too, and using "said" gives the reader zero confusion.

I don't know about you, but I hate reading a dialogue scene in a book where for two pages straight there is *no* dialogue attribution. When it's just straight dialogue on and on, without any break.

Dialogue attribution can help with this. My rule of thumb is usually five lines of dialogue. Five back-and-forths. At this point, if there's not a new "Jessica said" or "Daniel said," I have to ask myself why.

Using only "said" is also helpful because you don't want to get in trouble for using a strange word that makes the line of dialogue literally impossible. I used to see samples of like this one in writing workshops all the time. Lines like…

"He had the weirdest look on his face," Peter laughed.

You can't actually laugh a line of dialogue, right? I mean, I guess you could *try*, but it would be super awkward.

The same reason that a character weeping a line of dialogue also makes no sense. A character can weep while saying the line, but weeping the line itself is like… huh?

Dialogue attribution is something that takes a long time to master.

To decide when you should use it, and when you shouldn't. If you should put "Jane said" at the beginning of the line or at the end of it.

And to figure out how dialogue attribution will make the best possible rhythm for your sentences, too.

But there's something you don't have to master, and that's the simple rule of saying "said" in dialogue attribution whenever possible.

46. Why Backstory is So Important in Your Fiction Writing

Writing backstory into your fiction is often super tricky.

And I often find that backstory is one of the elements that improves considerably with lots of practice and time as a writer.

You might be really good right out of the gate with your dialogue. With your character development. With your chapter cliffhangers.

But backstory is like description. It needs to be there, but only some of the time. Write too much backstory, and the current reality of your story gets lost, and your reader might even lose interest. Write too little backstory, and your characters might become too one-dimensional, too stereotypical.

Even if your story is completely focused on a brief moment in time, you need *some* backstory. You need at least a hint of where these characters came from and what deep down makes them tick.

The way you integrate the backstory often makes or breaks your writing.

Stephen King recommends getting to the backstory as early as possible, and I mostly agree with that. If there's something important about your protagonist's backstory that will play a role in the narrative, don't introduce that information on page 367.

Don't introduce it on page 2 necessarily either but do introduce it early on. Have the reader thinking about that piece of the character's backstory, even it's just at the back of their mind. Doing so will allow the big moment that happens later to have a satisfying payoff.

The trick is finding the balance between too little backstory and too much backstory. Do you stop the story cold for a large paragraph to deliver backstory? I've seen this done well by authors, and I've seen it done not so well.

Personally, my favorite kind of backstory is woven into what's happening in the current narrative. I typically hate it when suddenly chapter 6 opens with a flashback that's filled with tons of backstory about the characters, and then we're not thrown back into the current reality until nine pages later.

I like, instead, when *one or two sentences* of backstory are delivered in the middle of a paragraph, or after a line of dialogue, or after a bit of description. Something that gives the reader a tiny little piece of backstory information that reveals something about the character.

Whatever you do, make sure you have a clear backstory for each of your major characters before you begin writing.

I like to write detailed character bios for my three or four main characters in each novel project I take on. Many of the details in these bios never find their way into the completed manuscript, and you know what? That's okay!

What's important is that you the author at least *know* the backstory. Have a handle on where each character came from, what makes them tick, why they do the things they do.

Knowing a lot more than you ever need to about each character will make your writing richer because then, once you know so much, you'll find yourself dropping little hints of backstory here and there throughout your manuscript. You'll be able to show your reader so much detail and insight about your characters!

Backstory is absolutely key to a great story, whether it's 40,000 words or 140,000 words. There's no excuse to avoid integrating backstory into your work. If you struggle with it, keep practicing. Don't think of backstory as merely flashback. Don't think of it as a way to stop the current story cold to deliver information to your reader.

Backstory should be delivered in a way that's surprising and informative and *entertaining* for the reader. Figure out how to integrate backstory, and you, my friend, are already ahead of the game.

47. However, Keep in Mind that Most Backstory isn't Interesting

Backstory should play some kind of role in your fiction writing.

It is absolutely important to have an aspect of backstory in your fiction, even in the most fast-moving of thrillers. It doesn't really matter what kind of genre you write in at the end of the day. Even if you're writing a real-time story told in first person that moves at crackerjack speed, there still needs to be a *little* bit of backstory somewhere.

That character didn't just suddenly land on Planet Earth in Chapter 1. Stuff happened to them before your story started. Big stuff and small stuff. Huge milestones and tiny moments that left significant impacts.

Backstory is such a tricky beast because it needs to be there in your work in some regard, but to overdo backstory might alienate many of your readers.

Sometimes backstory is so difficult to integrate you might be inclined to just *skip it altogether*. But don't. It does need to be there in a small capacity.

Just always keep in mind that most backstory isn't interesting.

Keeping this in mind has definitely helped me in terms of what backstories of my characters I include in my recent novels and what backstories I don't.

My novel *Monster Movie*, which got me a literary agent in 2017, had *so* much more backstory in its first few drafts. I stopped the story cold at times to explain why my main character Max was so passionate about filmmaking, and how his parents met, and what his dog Buster meant to him growing up. I included long passages of how he went to the movies with his dad. I included a huge flashback scene of how he discovered the films of his new favorite movie director on a dark and stormy night.

There was a lot of great writing in these moments, but as I continued revising the book for many months after I signed with the agent, I recognized that *most* of the backstory I included needed to go. Not because it wasn't relevant to the story I was telling. And not because the writing on my part was anything less than solid.

Most of it needed to go eventually… because it just *wasn't very interesting.*

To stop your story cold for backstory, you have to give us details that offer something unique. A fascinating image, perhaps. A quick anecdote about the protagonist that gives us deeper insight into them.

Once the urgency of the current narrative is lost, there needs to be a good reason for that backstory, and if there's isn't, if you're just loading up your chapter with various details of backstory you think the reader would like to know, you might be shooting yourself in the foot.

Especially when that backstory comes early in the narrative. Especially when it's page seven and you've unloaded huge block paragraphs of backstory upon your readers, most of whom will be annoyed by this.

You might not know what backstory is interesting or not, and that's okay.

Sometimes I find a particular bit of backstory about one of my characters fascinating, and it takes a bunch of readers to calmly let me know that backstory isn't fascinating *at all* but is in fact boring and brings the quality of the chapter down with its absurdness.

Okay, so this might not happen all the time, but something you should think about if you struggle with backstory is telling any beta readers who take a look at your book to keep an eye out for it. Tell them to make a note where backstory doesn't add much to the book, where backstory takes away from the urgency of the narrative.

Because, sadly, most backstory of someone's life isn't interesting. Especially in a work of fiction.

So stick to this important advice: present the bits and pieces of your characters' backstory that will hold a reader's interest, and then throw away the rest. Your novel will be better in the long run!

48. Why Symbolism in Your Writing Doesn't Need to be Difficult

There's so much to think about when you're drafting a novel.

You're thinking about making the narrative compelling and surprising, you're thinking about making your characters interesting, you're thinking about the quality of your prose. And of course you're thinking about your genre and the expectations that come with that.

I guarantee you that throughout the writing of my twenty novels over the last ten years, I have spent little to no time thinking about *symbolism.*

Symbolism is something I was forced to look for in the books I read in high school. As part of AP papers I would have to write about *Jane Eyre* and *The Scarlett Letter* and *A Tale of Two Cities.*

Shit, I'm an adult now. I don't have to think about symbolism in my writing!

And for the most part, you don't.

When you're drafting a novel, please don't fixate on how you're going to integrate symbolism into the narrative. That should not be at the forefront of your mind. That should not be something that even enters your head much as you go about writing your pages.

But should symbolism in your storytelling be forgotten about *entirely?*

Here's the deal: don't actively try to force symbolism into your writing, but if it's there, if there's something working as symbolism somewhere throughout your pages, then by all means, when you *revise*, polish that symbolism until it shines.

One of my favorite examples of symbolism in a story is the shirt within a shirt in *Brokeback Mountain.* Annie Proulx doesn't beat you over the head with the symbol. It's not all over every page. But it's certainly there, and it's polished enough that it lingers in the mind. And it's what makes that incredible final scene so emotionally resonating, both in the story version and the film version.

Stephen King has used some effective symbolism in his work as well.

Think of REDRUM in *The Shining*, which is such a powerful symbol because in a sense it means murder, but also means to *not* murder.

And think of the symbol of blood in *Carrie*. Blood when it comes to Carrie's period at the beginning. Blood when it comes to the pig's blood that's dumped on her at the prom. Blood when it comes to all the lives she slaughters that night.

Blood is so clearly a symbol in King's debut novel, but, again, he never beats you over the head with it. You don't really think of it as a symbol until you begin to analyze the story at a deeper level.

So don't panic, okay?

Don't think you need to have three amazing symbols in mind for your latest novel in the days before you start drafting.

If you do think of one early on, then great! Keep it at the back of your mind, and maybe try to work it in somewhere during the first draft, but feel free to leave that work for the revision instead.

And even if your symbolism is accidental, if there's something there that strikes you, polish it throughout your revisions to bring it out in a way that makes sense and that enriches the story even more for your readers.

Anything that makes your story better is always something you should consider no matter what.

49. Why Theme is So Important in Your Fiction Writing

It really is true: every book worth reading should be about *something*.

When I begin a new novel, theme is not at the top of my radar. I'm thinking about the protagonist—their wants, their dreams, and that thing that's going to keep them from achieving their dreams.

I'm thinking about the supporting characters, and the antagonist, and the central conflict, and specific scenes I want to write. I'm thinking about where the story begins and where the story ends.

To be perfectly honest, I don't put much thought into theme when I begin a new writing project. And you want to know why?

Because the theme *usually appears eventually*, after I've scanned every tree and have finally taken a step back to look at the entire forest.

The theme appears because any story I'm compelled to write, one that lives inside my mind month after month desperate to come out on the page, is *always* about something.

Sometimes the theme isn't super clear to me right away. Sometimes it takes until the third revision for the theme to finally break through. But it's always there.

If your book isn't at all about a larger idea, you're in trouble.

If the story's not about something that goes beyond your characters and your premise, then you might have to think long and hard if this is the project you want to write.

If all you're writing, for example, is a scary ghost story meant to freak the shit out of readers, and it's about *nothing else than that*, your novel might not reach as many readers as it could.

Because what makes books great is theme. What makes books great is something lingering under the surface of the narrative, of your protagonist's arc, that come to light in a way that strikes each reader differently.

When a book is entertaining, thrilling, surprising, *and* meaningful in some beautiful way?

That's where great stories come from. Those are the stories you turn to again and again.

The stories that aren't really about anything can be fun, can make the time pass fine for a few hours, but they won't leave any major impact on you. They won't be books that stay with you long after you've closed the final page.

Again, don't obsess over theme at the start of your project.

It absolutely doesn't hurt to know your theme at the beginning and keep it in the back of your mind as you draft your novel.

But don't fixate on theme either. You don't even have to know what your theme is as you start writing. Just make sure, always, that your book is about *something*. Beyond your genre. Beyond your premise. Beyond your main character.

And even it takes you until the revision process to understand exactly what your book is truly about, you'll be well on your way to crafting a compelling and memorable novel that no reader will want to miss.

50. Why You Need to be Careful with Research in Your Fiction Writing

Research can't be ignored when it comes to your fiction writing.

I mean, I guess it can if every novel you write is about things you already know about. If everything you write is sort of autobiographical and filled with moments and conflicts you see on a daily basis, then maybe you don't have to research much.

But a lot of the time, research plays a key role in the writing process before you begin drafting your novel. Certainly if there's an element of your story you have no idea about, then you need to do some research.

Sometimes research is as easy as taking a half-hour or an hour online and just reading different articles. I recently wrote a novel about a girl who has an allergy to water, so before I started the drafting process I spent a couple of weeks researching and taking notes about this very real allergy and how it has affected young people in recent years.

Sometimes research needs to go deeper, though. Sometimes you need to actually *talk* to somebody in the profession your main character has, for example.

Bottom line is that if you need to do research to make the book better, and to make the book makes sense, there's no good reason not to do it.

On the other hand, you do need to be careful about research when it comes to your fiction writing.

Why careful, exactly? Two reasons.

First, you could make research an excuse to *never write your novel.* You could spend months and months researching to the point of excess. When your writer friends ask what you're working on, you can say, "I'm researching for the new novel, it's going well, I'm learning a lot of fascinating things!"

This isn't good. When you're spending more time researching than actually writing, you're wasting your time.

Take a few weeks to research your next book, that's fine. But the research should end at a certain point, and the writing should begin.

The second reason you need to be careful?

Research should always stay as far in the background as possible in your fiction writing.

As soon as you start showing off your research and littering that information you found all over your manuscript, whether it's in description or thoughts or dialogue of your featured characters, you're making wrong choices.

A little bit of research on the page is okay. If there's a solid reason to include some of it here and there in your prose, that should be fine.

What you should be most concerned with, however, is *telling a compelling story*, and making sure the characters and conflict and growing tension take center stage, not the research you did before you started writing.

Research is definitely important in your fiction writing, but it should never replace the writing itself, and it should always, always, always stay as far in the background as possible.

51. If Research Intimidates You, Write the First Draft Anyway

There's something to be said about researching too much. But what if you don't want to research at all?

Okay, here's the deal—for the most part, I prefer not to do much research before I begin a new writing project. Yes, even if there are aspects to my latest project that I probably *should* research. Yes, even if I know at some point down the road I'm simply going to have to research one or more aspects of my story.

Some people spend too much time researching. I'm usually on the other end of the spectrum. I just want to *start writing.* I don't want to do any more brainstorming or outlining, or, yes, researching. I'm interested in my characters, in the central conflict and growing tension, in the emotion of my story.

Who the hell cares if I don't get every detail exactly right?

Sadly, the answer is a lot of your readers *will* care.

This is the part about avoiding research that can bite you in the ass as a writer. Especially if you're writing a novel set in the real world, you need to get your details right.

Because it's very well possible a wrong detail will break the magic for many of your readers. A reader will be enjoying your story, but then they will see an error in your description of a city or of a time period or of a car or of a style of clothing—and the magic is gone.

A few readers might even put down your book at this point and think, this author doesn't know what he's talking about, so I'm going to move onto a different story.

You. Do. Not. Want. This. To. Happen.

I know you might not want to hear it, but sooner or later you *will* need to do research on aspects of your story you don't know or understand. At some point of the process, research is vital to you doing the best job possible as a writer.

But here's the good news—you can do the research not sooner but later!

It is not essential that you necessarily conduct your research for your latest writing project *before* you start writing the opening sentence.

If you're like me, and don't necessarily like to research all that much, do what I do. Write the first draft to the best of your ability, putting in as much as you know in terms of the research aspect, making up a few things when you need to, and then do the research *later* in the revising process!

You don't even have to do research before the second draft. You could be even further along, be in the fourth or fifth draft, until you do any serious research.

I mean, I would get around to the research eventually. Don't have the entire novel super polished, only to then have to go back and cut long passages and add new researched information in a way that ruins some of the work you've already done.

But if you don't want to do research at the beginning, that's totally fine. Write the first draft, *finish* the first draft, and then get around to the research part later if you want to.

Just make sure you do the research at some point in time. Your readers will thank you for it.

52. Why Reality is So Important in Your Fiction Writing

You might think only literary stories set in our contemporary world need to be realistic.

You might think any research you have to do is for realistic stories, not necessarily genre stories or abnormal stories or paranormal stories.

If you're writing a science fiction story set in another galaxy, you might think you will be able to throw realism completely out the window. You're writing a story not set on Earth after all, so there are no rules, every facet of the reality can be made up, you can do anything!

Not so fast. The problem with throwing realism completely out the window is that your readers won't have anything to grab onto, they won't have anything that resembles the reality they currently know. Even if you're writing something super fantastical, you still need at least *some* sense of reality in your writing.

In fact, I think a sense of reality is even more important in a fantastical work than it necessarily is in a work of pure contemporary realism.

No sense of reality can bring a work of fiction down fast.

If chapter after chapter goes by and there's nothing that resembles real life we can grasp, it can be difficult to get involved in the story.

Put us on an oddly shaped spaceship. Introduce us to weird creatures we've never read about before. Write us images that are wholly original.

But give us *something* in terms of character, conflict, environment, relationships and tension and stakes, to get us invested emotionally.

And one way to do that is to stick close to realism, at least part of the time.

Research things you might need to research. Reference things we know in our world, at least a few things both tangible and intangible.

The great thing is that you can abandon reality once your reader has an emotional investment!

Within reason of course, but one super cool thing about storytelling is that if you can get your readers invested in your storyline and in your main characters, you gain yourself a little bit of freedom when it comes to reality in the rest of the narrative.

I think it takes a gifted writer to abandon reality completely. To just throw caution to the wind and make up so much along the way that there's nothing for the reader to recognize any longer.

I've never written a story like that. Well, I kind of did once, and it didn't work out the way I hoped it would. It's why, even in my more fantastical of stories, I maintain a sense of reality at almost all times.

Again, it doesn't matter what kind of fiction you write. Literary, horror, fantasy, science fiction, romance, mystery. Write in the genre you're passionate about and write in it well.

And always keep in the back of your mind that a sense of reality, at least in small doses, will make your writing soar all the more!

53. Why You Should Pay Attention to the Pacing of Your Novel

Here's the deal: faster pacing isn't necessarily better.

We live in an age where everything moves way too fast. Seemingly everyone has ADHD. It's hard to focus on one thing for more than thirty seconds. It's hard to pick up a book and read for longer than ten minutes without checking your phone. It's hard to watch a movie or TV at home, yes, without *constantly* checking your phone or taking breaks.

So the idea that you'll have more success as a writer if you pace your writing faster makes sense. Especially if you're writing fiction. Write a fast-paced, exciting story that never lets up, and you probably think you'll have a hit!

And maybe you *will* have a hit. Maybe fast pacing in your narrative writing works for you.

It's definitely worked for me throughout the years. I actually enjoy a fast pace for the most part. Especially when I'm writing a thriller, and the antagonist is clear, and the conflict has arisen, I like to just go bonkers with my pacing and make it so that the reader has no desire to ever put the book down until they reach THE END.

But you also need to take slow pacing into account as well.

If every scene and chapter of your novel moves faster and faster, without any let-up from the tension, your reader will become confused or tired or stressed out. You can't keep up the fast pace forever or you will absolutely burn out your reader.

I recently wrote a young adult thriller that has a super fast pace from beginning to end. I was inspired by *Mad Max: Fury Road* to write an entire novel that was essentially a car chase. From sentence one on, there's seriously no time for my protagonists to take a breath.

I love the fast pace of this novel, but in later revisions I've worked hard to slow down the pacing at least *a little bit* at times. I've tried to allow for scenes where the characters just talk to each other, as well as moments of sincere quiet in all that action.

Because a fast pace to a novel, no matter how well written or beautifully characterized, can only sustain itself for so long. You need to embrace the slow pace occasionally, too.

And don't ever think that slow pacing for the majority of a novel is a bad thing! Slow pacing is often my jam as a reader. I like thrillers that have a slow build for much of the novel, then has a fast-paced, exciting payoff at the end. Slow burns almost always leave me satisfied.

What will leave readers satisfied more than anything? Stories with a mix of slow pace and fast pace.

When you never really know what's going to come next in that narrative. An action scene. A moment of quiet reflection. When *anything* can happen at any moment, now that's the excitement of a stellar work of fiction.

Move fast all the time, and your reader will get exhausted. Move slow all the time, and yes, your reader will likely get bored and potentially put down the book.

If you incorporate a mix of fast pacing and slow pacing, you can write something incredible.

Finding the right rhythm to your pacing takes time. You won't nail it on your first story or novel. It might even take years and years of practice.

But keep working on the pacing. You will get better at it eventually.

Have both the fast and the slow, and you'll be well on your way to finding more success in your fiction.

54. Write a Reader-Friendly Story if You Want to be Successful

There are so many reasons to write.

To get something off your chest. To explore your fears, your dreams, your imagination. To get a story written down you feel the world simply needs to read.

When it comes to your fiction writing, you can write whatever you want. If gruesome horror stories are your jam, go for it. If a cozy mystery makes you happy, then by all means, write fifty of them. If you like to write erotica, or westerns, or science fiction, or *all three*, get started today and not tomorrow.

Just keep writing no matter what. Write, write, write to your heart's content!

There are so many reasons to write, and there are also so many things to keep in mind before, during, and after your writing sessions. You want to think about your story and how it progresses. You want to think about your characters and how they develop. You want to think about pacing, structure, themes.

Yes, I know, there's *so damn much* to keep in mind.

But one other thing you should think about as you navigate the world of fiction writing?

Make sure your story is reader-friendly.

Now this is not the same thing as having your story ready for readers in terms of *revision* and *proofreading* and things like that. No matter what you write, yes, it should be reasonably revised and proofread and typo-free and all that good stuff.

What reader-friendly means is that your story should be *compelling for the average reader*. It should *entertain* the average reader. There should be something about your story that captivates people.

This is why genre is such a great place to work in when you're a writer. To write specifically thrillers, or military novels, or romance books. There are millions of readers out there for each particular major genre, after all.

If you want to write strictly literary novels, or maybe blend genres into something unique, then you might find it harder for your stories to be reader-friendly, and you need to be prepared for that. If you want to write something super complex and weird and off-the-wall strange, it will be all the more difficult to get readers to be open to your story.

This is not to say that your stories should ever be formulaic.

You might think of writing reader-friendly stories to mean that you need to be predictable, formulaic, obvious. Give the readers what they want and everyone will be happy!

Not so fast. It's not enough to just give readers exactly what they want. That might work for a story or two, but your writing will get stale after awhile, and no potential reader of yours is going to want that.

What you should do instead is write stories that are reasonably reader-friendly, with a premise and characters and themes that can translate to great reader interest, while at the same time delivering something every time that is original, unique… *and totally mind-blowing.*

You want to write a story will at least somewhat meet the readers' expectations while at the same time give them something new and amazing. Something entirely unexpected!

So, yes, you need to think of both extremes while writing your novel.

Keep your readers' expectations in mind on one end of the spectrum but do your own thing on the other end of the spectrum.

Don't waste your time writing something nobody will ever want to read.

However, don't write something that necessarily everybody in the world will want to read either.

Remember that you can't please *all* of the readers *all* the time, but, if you want to be a successful writer, you should try to please *most* of your readers *most* of the time.

So write what you love, write in the genre you're passionate about, make sure your stories are at least somewhat reader-friendly.

And at the same time don't be afraid to take risks.

55. 3 Reasons Why You Need to Stick with Your Latest Writing Project

The scariest moment is always right before you start.

Staring at that first blank page, especially of a novel, is so daunting and intimidating and terrifying, it's a wonder any of us are able to begin, continue writing, and actually complete any writing of value.

And I do think one thing people struggle with is the doubt that they can write a novel, the doubt that they'll ever be able to actually start it and push forward chapter by chapter.

The trick is finding a story and characters that you love and then finding a specific time each day to sit down and write it. The first task you have is *getting started*. Don't think about the immensity of the novel. Don't think about how long it might necessarily take you to reach the end of it.

In twenty novels, I have never focused on or obsessed over the day in the future I might finish the book. I rarely even think of my stories as novels while I'm writing. Because what I do is focus on the *amount of words I want to reach that day*, not the amount of words I want to reach over many weeks and months.

Once you learn to focus on the work of the current day, and not get intimidated by the novel as a whole, you will find your rhythm and success in novel writing.

Get started, yes, that's the first part. But you need to keep going. Don't stop and start a second project. Don't take a year-long break because the story got too hard.

Here are three reasons why you should keep sticking with your latest project…

1. A messy first draft is a lot more useful than a beautifully written draft that's only halfway done.

If there's one thing I want you to take away from this book, it's exactly that. Keep writing. *Finish the thing.*

You can't do anything with half a novel. You can't revise pages that haven't been written yet.

Get to the end however you can. Maybe you like to write short first drafts and then build on what you already have. Maybe you want to go long (like I always do) and then cut back.

The best reason possible to stick with your latest writing project is that the more time you dedicate to finishing it and then revising it later is the best chance you have at success in your writing career. Because you might be able to sell your novel one day or get a literary agent for it.

You can't query a novel until it's all done, remember that, and you shouldn't query it until it's gone through extensive revisions. Finish your novel, stick with it for the long haul, and you have a better shot at something happening with that story you love.

2. Finishing your current project will give you the confidence to complete other projects.

I spent a decade wondering if I could actually write a novel. Since I was a boy I always saw myself as a published author, as someone who could write books one day, and as early as 1999 I entertained the idea of writing a novel. I was fourteen at the time, and boy, that book would have sucked hard.

But I thought about it for a long, long time. Every time I walked through a bookstore I thought about trying to write a novel. I just didn't think I could ever do it. I could write screenplays but not novels. I didn't have the patience to write an entire novel. I didn't feel I had the talent for it.

It wasn't until I re-read Stephen King's *On Writing: A Memoir of the Craft* sometime in 2009 and had a story idea I loved that I thought would work better in novel form than in screenplay form that I decided to give it a shot. So one day in April 2010 I started writing my first novel, and I didn't stop until I reached the end.

That moment I wrote the final sentence of my first novel was electrifying. Because I had finished a novel, of course. But also because I realized I could do it *again*. Once you finish one novel, you get the confidence to start another project in the months to come and you're able to finish that one, too. And the next one. And the next one after that.

You don't want to only write one novel in your life, right? You want to write several I hope. And sticking with one project long enough to see it through to its final page will help you understand that writing novels is do-able. Especially if you go about them the right way and figure out sooner than later that they're not as scary as you might have previously thought.

3. Writing the book really does get easier as you go along.

The scariest part is the beginning, when there are no words on the page. But I'm telling you, at least from my experience, as soon as you finish chapter one, things slowly begin to get easier.

One, because you have found your way into the story and now you can start having fun developing your plot and characters. And two, because the deeper into your manuscript you get, the more you begin to learn and understand more about your characters and the world of your story.

One reason why first drafts are messy is that you don't always know *everything* about your story and characters when you begin writing (at least I don't), and so often great ideas come while I'm writing while I'm thinking about my story throughout the day.

So by the time I reach the last page I'm a lot more informed about things than I was in the beginning. And when I get going on my second draft and especially my third and fourth drafts, I'm able to add, cut, and revise things that give the illusion to whomever eventually reads the project later that *I knew what I was doing all along.*

You should always try to complete any writing project you begin, I truly believe that.

Sure, sometimes there's the rare circumstance when you should take a break from your novel or possibly abandon it completely.

But again, that is a *rare* circumstance. I've certainly started projects that took me in directions I didn't expect, and I've messed up chunks of a few of my books where I had to cut lots and lots of scenes and chapters in later drafts.

The truth of the matter is this: you will have success in your fiction writing career, at least eventually, *if you finish things.* If you begin projects, write your heart out, and complete them.

Feel free to take a break halfway through if you absolutely need to, but in as many cases as possible, go back to those projects and take them all the way to the end.

One more time, ready? A messy first draft that's finished is way more useful than an extremely well-written draft that's only halfway done.

Never forget it!

56. Never Throw Your Writing in the Trash

It may be the most famous Stephen King story of them all.

He got the idea for *Carrie*, started writing the story, and immediately found himself struggling. He didn't know anything about high school girls. He didn't identify with the protagonist.

The writing got hard, and he got frustrated, and one day he grabbed the pages he'd typed so far of *Carrie* and threw them in the trash.

Later on, he came home from a day of teaching to find the pages retrieved from the wastebasket by his wife, Tabitha. She had read what he'd written so far, and she not only liked it but was interested to see where the story went next. "You have something here," she said to Stephen.

Isn't it weird to think what might have happened if Tabitha King didn't save the pages from the trash can, if Stephen didn't ever finish *Carrie*? I think it's pretty safe to say he would have been a publishing sensation at some point, maybe not with *Carrie* but with *'Salem's Lot* or something else.

But also… maybe he wouldn't have. No *Carrie* might have set him back a few extra years, might have not allowed for interest in his other novels. You just never know.

The universe aligned with Stephen King that day when Tabitha just happened to peer inside the waste basket and retrieve the pages of *Carrie*. The book went on to be

---

published, become a sensation, be turned into a blockbuster horror film. And it made King a boatload of cash.

The moral of this story may be simple, may be obvious, but it's essential…

Don't. Throw. Any. Of. Your. Writing. Away.

Even your oldest, worst fiction. Even your utter crap.

Now this is a little easier to do in 2020 than it was in the early 1970s. When you write everything on a typewriter, it's easier to lose those loose pages. It's easier to misplace that story you wrote two years ago and forgot where you put it.

When you have everything on your computer, it's always there. As long as your system doesn't crash and you don't drop your fifteen-year-old file into the trash icon, you're probably fine.

So if all of your writing is resting soundly on your harddrive somewhere, I'd like to take this advice a step further: copy and paste all your years' worth of short stories, novels, poetry into a specific folder that contains everything. Yep, everything!

You *never know* what piece might speak to you in the moment. Once in a while, when I have time, I'll pull up an old unpublished story I haven't looked at in a few years, and I'll spend an afternoon revising it, cleaning it up, adding new dialogue, expanding the beginning and ending.

Twice I have done this, sent it out, and almost immediately *gotten the piece published*. Again, you just never know.

At the very least, reading through some of your old work might spark an idea for a newer piece.

It might spark an idea for something with a similar concept that's maybe more complex, more involving. There is a creepy monster story I wrote in sixth grade I re-read on a rainy Sunday, and I instantly realized there was a nugget of a great story there I could turn into a novel. And in 2019, I finally did!

This is why I save everything. It's in my nature. Even if you don't look at something for ten years or longer, there might be that lazy Sunday you want to pull it out again and see if there's anything there you can use for a later project.

This goes for old short stories, and, yes, this goes for writing that's been deleted from earlier drafts of your novels.

You. Just. Never. Know.

So don't panic if you have to cut big chunks from your novel, and don't feel like those old unpublished stories you wrote at the beginning of your career should go in the trash, never to be seen again.

Hold onto your writing, okay? You'll be glad you did.

57. The 5 Steps You Need to Take to Complete Your Novel

Writing your first novel is an ambitious undertaking that might seem a little scary at first. But if you have a really good idea and feel in your heart and soul that this is something you must do, then you simply have to write it.

Here are five steps to complete your first novel…

1. Go with the Idea and Genre You're Most Passionate About.

Odds are you have more than one idea in your head. You might have five or six in a variety of genres.

You know what? Go with the one that excites you the most, and the one that you feel most qualified to write about.

If you've worked in law for the last five years and have a great idea about a law thriller, that might be the better idea to go with than a science fiction saga about gender politics.

2. Read, Read, Read, Read, Read.

Quentin Tarantino didn't go to film school to train himself to make movies; the man watched lots and lots of movies instead.

It's the same with writing fiction. Your passion and determination may get you through writing your first novel, but if you don't find time to read books, it's going to show in your writing. You don't want to copy what other authors are doing, but you want to *learn* from what styles and ways that published authors write.

Feel free to read only in the genre you're looking to write in, or a mix of many. Just read!

3. Pick a Time and Write At Least Five Days A Week.

Even if you're feeling writer's block, you still need to get your butt in the chair and write. Even if what you write for the next hour is crap, it will get your brain working, and you will start creating better work.

Most first-time writers don't have the luxury of time. You might have to get up two hours earlier in the morning or stay up three hours past your bedtime. If you really want to write, you're going to have to make some sacrifices, and the main one just might be your hours of sleep.

4. Stick to a Word Count.

Feel free to write 2,000 words a day. Or 200. The great thing about writing is re-writing. Just get those words down, get from chapter one to chapter twenty-seven, and *finish the book.*

There will be good days and bad days. Don't freak out those first few days. You might feel like you're climbing Mount Everest. Don't look too far in the future. Just focus on today. Just focus on the words you're putting on the page *today.*

And before you'll know it, you'll be writing your last sentence.

5. Print Out Your Manuscript and Put it in a Drawer.

Congratulations! It took a few weeks or a few months, but you finished your novel! You did it! Celebrate and print out your manuscript. Whether it's 50,000 words or 150,000 words, you've accomplished a huge feat.

Now the last step in this part of your journey is to put your book in a drawer and don't pull it back out for at least four to six weeks. Revision will be your next step, but you want to approach the book as a reader, not a writer. Let the book breathe out of sight for a few weeks.

And then, and *only* then, the crucial revising stages will begin.

58. Here's One Easy Way to Finish Your Novel Quickly

You might feel like there's no easy way to finish your novel.

There are so many ways to write a novel, after all.

I've talked about how if you're pressed for time, you can always find ten to twenty minutes a day and write a little bit. If you write 200 words a day, you can complete a novel in one year!

But what if you want to get a first draft of your novel completed quickly and not slowly? What if you could finish your novel in a few weeks time, not a few months time?

I often spend a year or longer revising my novel projects, but I always write the first draft quickly. In four to six weeks typically. Only in rare cases longer than eight weeks.

Even if you have a full-time job, it can be done. You don't have to spend a long year slowly writing here and there before you reach the end.

Here's one easy way to finish your novel quickly…

Write 500 words in thirty-minute sprints.

This is the big one. Especially if you have little time to devote to your project every day.

When I write a novel, I often write 2,000 words a day. 2,000 words is a lot, so something that helps me get started is not look at the session as 2,000 words but as four thirty-minute sprints of 500 words.

There's something about this weird way of thinking that always helps me get through the writing session not just well but *fast.*

I'll sit down at, say, 10am. And I almost always will be done with my writing for the day by 12pm, as long as there are no distractions.

I give myself between 10am and 10:30am to reach 500 new words. Sometimes, when I'm on a roll, I can get there in fifteen to twenty minutes. And if that happens? I give myself a ten-minute break!

I'll look at the clock. It says 10:20. And I get to goof off for exactly ten minutes.

Then at 10:30 on the dot, I start the second thirty-minute sprint. If I finish before 11am, I get another brief moment to relax. Maybe get a snack. Maybe surf a couple websites. Maybe check my e-mail. But only after I've reached another 500 words.

Then I move onto the third sprint, and then the fourth sprint. Voila, in two hours typically I've written 2,000 new words!

Now if you don't actually *have* two hours… no problem.

If you need to, find four thirty-minute sprints throughout your day!

I typically write my 2,000 words in two straight hours, and if you're able to write that way, I recommend it. It's easier to get into a groove when you stay with your writing in one period of the day rather than several.

However, what's neat about the sprints idea is that you can split it into two parts if you want—one hour of two sprints in the morning, and one hour of two springs at night!

You can even split it into four sprints if you want. One in the morning, one at lunchtime, one in the evening, and one late at night.

I wouldn't necessarily advise that, but if your time is limited, and you want to finish your first draft quickly, then go for it.

One other thing to remember? It's okay if you can't reach 500 words in thirty minutes. I've had days where I can only get 200–300 words in thirty minutes. I've had days where I sat there staring at the screen for thirty minutes, no words achieved at all!

This will happen sometimes. Don't beat yourself up over it. If you don't get 2,000 words a day, it's not the end of the world. If you only get to two of your sprints instead of four, there's no need to panic.

But I guarantee you, when you start looking at the writing of your novel in thirty-minute sprints, you will start writing more.

And you'll finish your novel sooner rather than later!

59. Why You Should Never Share the First Draft of Your Novel

As you write the first draft of your novel, there are going to be moments when you want to show it to someone.

It's not going to happen every day, trust me. There will be days where everything you put down on the page is total shit. There will be days where you struggle just to get the words down at all. These are not going to be the days you want to share *anything*.

But there will be occasional moments when the writing is going really, really well. When the last two scenes you wrote are freaking awesome, and you're walking away from the laptop smiling and cheering for your talented self.

You'll think to yourself, *I have to show this to someone, I have to share this right now!*

Yes, that impulse will come here and there when you're working on the first draft of your novel. Novels take forever to draft, after all. Sometimes a month if you're really fast, but often two months or longer. It can be hard to write your fiction week after week and not show at least a page or two to *somebody*.

But trust me, you need to resist this impulse.

Patience is such a key part of success in writing. Patience, and hard work, will make you stand out from the crowd.

And being patient about showing people your writing will be the best decision you make in the long run. Because no matter how amazing you think the pages you drafted yesterday are, no matter how fantastic chapter 15 is in every way, it's still important that you not show it to anyone yet.

Why?

One, the scene is probably not as great as you think it is.

It's probably filled with typos and misspellings and confusing paragraphs and awkward sentences that you won't ever notice until the second draft, maybe even the third.

Character motivations may not be super clear either. Why share your work until it's ready?

Two, what's to gain from sharing pages of your work-in-progress anyway?

Let's say that your chapter 1 is amazing. No typos, no misspellings. It flows, it's great, it works. You share that chapter with a friend or family member or writer you admire, and that person says, fantastic! I love this! I want to read more!

Then what? Do you show them *everything*? What if they love the first few chapters, to the point where you become too intimidated and self-conscious to write the rest of the book?

Three, what's most important, yes, is that you finish the first draft.

The whole point of the first draft is to get the story down as best you can… and *finish it.* I keep saying this because it's one of the most important things you can learn as a novel writer.

I've met so many talented writers over the years who write beautiful prose and wonderful stories and three-dimensional characters… but never finish a goddamn thing.

There's so much more to do with a mediocre first draft of a novel than an absolutely sublime novel that never gets finished. Your goal in writing a novel is not to share pages you like with others as you're going along but to keep that first draft to yourself and do the best you can with it until you reach the final page.

And when you finally finish that first draft, still resist the impulse to share your work.

It's done, it's finally done after months of work, so you're naturally going to want to hand the manuscript over to somebody. A partner, a best friend, a family member.

Don't do it. I'm telling you, *do not do it!*

Instead, put that first draft in the drawer for at least a month, if not six weeks or longer, and let it rest. Let it just sit there. And don't let anyone read a word of it.

Then after that time has passed, take the manuscript out of the drawer and start your second draft. I guarantee that you will be so thankful you never showed anyone that first draft. Because you will see hundreds of mistakes in your manuscript. You will fix most of them. You will make that book better.

And when you finish your *third* draft, then and only then should you show your novel to anyone.

If you want to be a successful writer, you need to wait it out.

Show your work to others when it's 80% there, 90% there, not when it's 30% or 40%. You want people to look at your work when the story is exciting and believable, and your characters make sense, and the prose is as polished as you can possibly make it.

You want people to help make your good manuscript *great.* You don't want them to look at your poor manuscript and then never want to read another word you put down again.

Enjoy the process. Write the novel for you at first. Don't rush. Don't feel like you need to show it to anyone, not for awhile.

The time will come, I promise. You just need to be patient.

60. Why You Need to Celebrate When You Finish Your Novel

There truly is nothing like completing the first draft of a novel.

I still remember when I finished my first book. It was the end of May 2010. I had been wanting to write a novel for years. There were so many times I would walk around Barnes & Noble wishing I could one day have a book on the shelf.

But writing a novel just seemed too hard. I figured I would burn out after a week or two and never finish it.

Finally, in the spring of 2010, when I was tired of writing screenplays and wanted a new challenge, I thought up a story about a casting director I wanted to tell in novel form, and I was bound and determined to write the whole thing no matter what.

I followed Stephen King's advice. 2,000 words a day every day. I worked a full-time job from 9am to 7:30pm so I wrote at night, usually from about 10pm to 1am. I wrote every day for six weeks, and then at the end of May I had a 106,000-word first draft of a novel.

It's been ten years, and I *still* remember that feeling. I didn't move at first. I just stared in awe at the screen. I had written that final scene the way I wanted and then typed THE END, on page 463. I couldn't believe it. I had finished a novel.

What did I do next? Once I finally was able to blink a few times and recognize the enormity of what I had just accomplished?

I printed out the pages, grabbed a pen, and started marking up the first page of the manuscript.

Yes, I forgot a few crucial parts about what to do when you complete a novel.

I followed King's book *On Writing* so closely that I didn't let the manuscript rest for six weeks or longer, like he suggests. I was just so excited I couldn't wait a single minute before starting the second draft.

I remember thinking to myself, maybe if I start revising now, I can pitch the novel to literary agents later in the summer!

Which I did. My first queries went out in July. Less than *two months* after I completed my first draft—a big no-no I would never do today.

I needed to let that novel rest for a few weeks. At least two weeks. At least a weekend! Jeez, I couldn't even bother to take a breath for grabbing a pen and marking up that opening page.

When you don't let your manuscript rest, you remain way too close to the material, to the characters. You can't really judge the manuscript in a way that's helpful, so what you end up doing is just copyediting the words that are already there.

So I didn't put my novel in the drawer for a month or longer, that was one mistake. What was my other mistake?

I didn't take the time to celebrate.

This was a huge deal. After years of thinking about writing a novel, hoping it might happen one day, I actually sat down at my laptop for six weeks, and I did it. I wrote an entire novel to the best of my ability.

I remember finishing it on a Friday, too. Right before a long weekend! And I honestly have no recollection of celebrating at all. I didn't celebrate with my friends or my family. I think I might have called my mom to tell her I finished a book, but that was about it.

I was so obsessed with revising the novel right away and pitching the book to literary agents that I didn't take a moment to step back and celebrate what I'd done.

It was a major accomplishment many had tried and failed to do before me. A major accomplishment that served as proof I could write a novel and write many *more* novels.

I should have taken my friends out to dinner that night. I should have bought myself something nice. I should have enjoyed life to the fullest the next few days.

Instead, I just focused on the next step of the process right away, which I realize now was the worst thing I could have done.

So when you finish your novel, please don't forget to celebrate!

It doesn't have to be a huge celebration. You don't have to throw a party for yourself and invite 500 people.

But yes, please, celebrate! Put the first draft of your novel in the drawer and take the time to bask in the glory of what you just accomplished. You finished a novel. You created something from scratch, something that didn't exist and now does, that came out of your imagination and is now in the world.

So have some champagne, treat yourself to a nice dinner, tell your friends and family what you achieved, and *enjoy yourself*. The revision of your novel is super important, but that part can come later.

Right now? Take the time to celebrate. You'll be glad you did!

All right, awesome, you've finished the first draft, and you've celebrated long enough. What happens next? Let's move onto maybe the most important part of all… revising and editing!

REVISING & EDITING

61. Why Revision is Key if You Want to be a Successful Writer

Revision is everything if you want to be a writer.

Revision is the difference between a good manuscript and a great manuscript. Revision is the difference between signing with a literary agent and being swiftly rejected by literary agents. Revision is the difference between an unpublished novel and a published novel.

At the end of the day, if you don't put in the work at the revising stage, you're never going to make it as a writer.

Every one of my twenty novels has gone through its own stages of revision, some on the shorter end and some on the higher end. An adult novel I wrote a few years ago that wasn't working very well I stopped at draft number two, and I have yet to return to it. My first few novels I wrote I did three or four drafts.

But I've done many, many drafts for most of my novels.

My first ever middle grade novel I wrote in 2014 went through nine drafts before I sadly abandoned it.

My MFA thesis novel I've been working on since 2017 has received twelve drafts, one of which completely gutted and restructured the middle 100 pages of the book.

My newest middle grade novel went through, wait for it, sixteen drafts total. Sixteen drafts over a four-year period!

Unfortunately, whether or not you're a good reviser does not come down to how many drafts of your novel you do or don't do. Just because you did sixteen drafts of your book doesn't necessarily mean it's perfect and ready.

There are different kinds of revision, and I've done them all.

There's a *major* revision, where you find yourself cutting characters and chapters and rewriting new scenes and restructuring so much of your book. I've done this on each of my last five novels. This kind of revision often takes six to eight weeks and lots of hard work and dedication.

There's a *minor* revision, where you're still cutting and adding scenes, re-arranging the occasional chapter, and working on your pacing and flow. This kind of revision usually takes place after a major revision, when I've done lots of great work but still have a few troublesome places I need to continue working on. This draft might take anywhere from four to six weeks.

And then there's what I like to call the *copyedit* revision, which I do often, especially when I'm lazy. The copyedit revision is where you basically go through your novel chapter by chapter and revise your work at the line-level, re-writing sentences and deleting typos and coming up with better transitions, things like that. Basically tinkering with *the words.* This kind of revision is by no means a bad thing, and it's likely necessary at some point.

However, a copyedit revision is never enough, especially at the beginning of the revising process. You can't just write the first draft of your novel to the best of your ability and then do a copyedit draft and then say, okay, I'm done! Let's query literary agents!

Don't worry if you've done this. I've certainly done it before. I've written novels in the past that I thought were 90% there on the first draft, and then after two more copyedit revisions, I sent them out and waited for the publishing contract to arrive at my doorstep.

What I've learned is that until you seek a few fresh pairs of eyes for your manuscript and get some valuable feedback, your book isn't yet at the end stage of revision.

You might think the book is awesome, but until you get some trusted beta readers, whether it be your writer friends or a literary agent or even strangers interested in your story, you can't be fully confident that your work is ready.

Now, if three people or more look at your manuscript and all tell you the same thing—that it's working really well— then maybe you do have a draft that needs little work. But if three or more people give you constructive criticism that will in every way make your novel better, you need to take that criticism into account.

If you ignore the criticism, and you just plow forward with one more copyedit revision before sending it out, you haven't done the necessary work. You've essentially skipped an important step in order to reach the end game.

You might think you've saved yourself a month or more of time, but in the end, when your book doesn't sell or you don't sign with a literary agent, you'll recognize that the time you actually wasted was all those months you spent writing the first and second and third drafts.

Trust me, I've learned this the hard way.

It's better for you to take the necessary time during revision to make your book the absolute best it can be, whether that be two more months or six more months or whatever, than to get your book to 80% and then stop there.

If you believe in your novel, if you think you've written a story that is truly exceptional, you need to put in the extra work when you revise.

And sometimes you will get frustrated. And sometimes you will think, enough already. You'll be tired of looking at the same words over and over. You'll want to move on to something else, anything else!

But do the work, anyway. In the long run, your novel will be so much better for it, and you will become a stronger, more confident, and more successful writer!

62. Why Your Writing Improves When You Take Significant Breaks

Wait—shouldn't you work on a project until it's 100% done?

It seems so contradictory, doesn't it? To write well, you have to allow for periods of no writing, or, better yet, a halt to the writing of your current project and the beginning of writing something completely different.

It sounds unnecessary. And sometimes you love a project so much the thought of abandoning it for a month or longer seems impossible.

But trust me. This works.

The first half of the novels I would work on nearly every day for months, through revision one, revision two, and so on, until I got the manuscript to its best possible place. I queried these novels… and then nothing happened.

My problem was that I wasn't really revising the books. I was so close to the story and to the characters that the revisions were basically glorified copy-editing—changing words and sentences around—but never really addressing problems with the bigger picture.

So yes, to be a writer, you need to take breaks!

What's changed me a lot the past few years is taking long breaks from my works-in-progress so that when I return to them I read them with fresh eyes.

I've made a practice of late to write a first draft of a novel, let it rest for at least four weeks (if not longer), and during that break time, write a new short story. I'll do this after the second draft, too. And the third. And the fourth.

You should try to turn your attention to a new creative project while your draft is resting, preferably something different from your novel. Maybe a story of a different genre. Or a non-fiction piece. Or a group of poems. You want to find *something* to keep your creative juices flowing at the same you're able to remove yourself from the world of your latest novel.

I wouldn't be where I am today if I kept up the practice of never giving myself breaks. I'd probably still be perfecting a previous manuscript that had no shot at being represented by a literary agent.

But is a four week break enough?

In his craft book *On Writing*, a craft book I read once a year, Stephen King recommends you take at least *six weeks* between drafts.

This is even better than four weeks, but I do still think a month is enough to do the job. That's enough time to keep you excited about the next revision of your work-in-progress while you still have room to play in a different creative project.

Granted, I understand you might not always have the luxury to rest between drafts. Sometimes there are deadlines in the publishing world, like when you're under contract and have only so many days to get your manuscript to an editor.

But if you do have the luxury of time, take breaks between drafts, at least four weeks, if not longer. I once let a novel of mine sit for fourteen *months*, and when I came back to it, it was like looking at the work of a different writer—I was able to approach the book as a ruthless editor, and I had a blast.

You probably won't have fourteen months, but at least give yourself a few weeks, and, trust me, your fiction will be all the better for it.

63. Why Your Second Draft Needs to be Shorter

In the first draft, go as long as you want.

Within reason, of course. But don't obsess over the length of your novel when you're writing the first draft. Tell yourself the story. Write the scenes you want to write. The first draft is not the time to be shy. Attack your story in the best way you can.

Every good idea, every character interaction that adds something to the story, put it in there. Better to add it to the first draft and cut it later than have to write a new scene from scratch in the months to come.

Sometimes that does happen, of course. I'll be on the fifth or sixth draft of a novel and there I am writing a brand new scene that never existed in the narrative before. The deeper you're in your revisions, the harder it is to write new content because so much of the book is now polished, while that new scene you just wrote is still only a first draft.

So—again, within reason—write the first draft as long as you want. Make it 120,000 words if that's what you feel you need to do.

(Although, when it comes to novels, do be aware of average word counts for your genre and/or market. If you're writing a contemporary middle grade novel, it's not in your best interest to write a 120,000-word first draft. That's just wasting time in the long run.)

Remember the most important thing about a first draft is that you finished it. Whether you come in on the short end or the long end, finishing the thing is what truly counts.

But whenever possible, you should try to finish a first draft of a novel *a little bit* on the long end. Why?

Because then you can spend time on the second draft trimming the fat of your manuscript, preferably by about 10%.

A big reason why I like to go a little long in the first draft of a novel is that I always prefer to cut, cut, cut. Trim, trim, trim. I like to look at a scene, look at a page, and see what can go.

I am a ruthless editor of my own work. I have been known to cut 5,000 words, 10,000 words, even sometimes up to 20,000 words easily, without remorse, without crying my eyes out over all those missing words I may have wasted my time on in that first draft.

Cutting is one of the prime things I like to do in the second draft of a novel. I like to read it through first without any revision at all, and then I spend three to four weeks going through the book chapter by chapter and what I mostly do during this time is edit things out.

You can't be precious about your words in a manuscript. You have to include the words that need to be there, that make your story its best, and then you have to remove the words that bring your story down.

Cutting 10% from the first draft is a good marker. Sure, it might be 5% or 8% or maybe even 15% or more depending on how long you went. But I don't believe you should necessarily use the second draft of any writing project to *add* a whole lot. You should be using it to cut.

Instead, use the third, fourth, and fifth drafts to add material. You will have time down the road to add that one scene you forgot to include in the first draft or build upon your description and imagery.

In the second draft, you should be reading through your manuscript slowly, taking notes about what elements of your story and characters are working and what aren't. Any scene that's confusing. Any exchange of dialogue that could use some work.

Let me make this very clear—you do not need to fix every single thing in the second draft.

Unless you're a genius, you're not going to get everything right in the first draft, and you certainly won't get everything right in the second draft either.

Use the second draft for taking notes on what needs improvement, on what you could potentially add in the drafts to come, and use it to cut your manuscript down by, on average, 10%.

If the first draft of your novel comes in at 100,000 words, then aim for 90,000 words for the second draft.

No matter what stage of the revising process you're in, you should always be thinking about what you can cut. If it doesn't have to be there… then it needs to go!

Even if you love the scene. Even if you love the character. If it's not adding anything, you might have to make the tough decision of deleting it from the manuscript.

At the very least, try to cut around 10% in that second draft. It's a great rule to live by to be a successful writer!

64. Why You Need to Read Your Chapters Twice When You Revise

———

Revision is an absolutely crucial part of the writing process.

There's simply no way you'll ever be successful if you don't revise your work and revise it often. Writing the first draft of anything is essentially just telling yourself the story. Revising the work is the time where you actually *shape* your story and improve it to a place where people will be able to read it.

There are of course so many ways to revise. Different people have different kinds of advice for this part of the process.

In ten years of writing novels, I've tried pretty much *everything* when it comes to revision…

1. Printing out every page of the work and making handwritten notes

For my first few books, I actually printed out the first draft and spent weeks making handwritten notes on the pages.

I do still think there's a noticeable difference between reading your words on the printed page and reading your words on a computer screen.

The problem with this method is that it takes *forever* to then transfer all the changes back to the computer screen, and after a few years, I (sadly) stopped doing this.

I still like to occasionally print out a draft of my work and read it hardcopy, but for revision, I lately stick to the words on the screen.

2. Letting the manuscript rest for at least four weeks

Another revision method I enact whenever possible is to let four weeks or longer pass between drafts, whether it's the second draft or the tenth draft.

As I discussed before, when you let a manuscript rest for a long, long time, you can really see in total clarity what's working and what isn't.

Whether it's a weekend or a year between drafts, remember to figure out your goals for the next draft. You don't want to waste your time doing the same thing on the next revision that you did on the previous one.

3. Sending your work to beta readers for feedback

I'm a big believer in doing two major revisions, then sending the manuscript to four or five people to get their feedback. This gives you another break from the novel, and when you return for the fourth draft, you have new insight into what's working and what isn't in the story.

You can certainly send out your fourth draft instead, or maybe your fifth draft. But eventually you do need to send your novel out, or otherwise you might just be dotting the i's and crossing the t's and not really fixing elements of your manuscript that still need work.

One other thing I believe in strongly when it comes to each round of revising a novel in particular?

You should read your chapters *twice* in each revision, not just once.

Something I started doing about five years ago I find especially helpful is reading through my chapters twice upon every revision.

What I mean by that is this… revise a chapter one day. And then the next day, revise that same chapter again, while *also* moving on to a new chapter you haven't looked at yet. And so on, and so forth.

How does this process help exactly?

1. It gives you two chances to make changes in each chapter, not just one. Instead of reading through a chapter once and then returning to it in, oh, two or three *months*, I read through it twice, which gives me peace of mind that I've done, at this moment in time, everything I wanted to do to that particular section of the story. It's in a sense like doing two drafts in one.

2. Reading through the chapter a second time helps you find any mistakes you might have made the day before. When you re-write a sentence, cut a paragraph, add a line of dialogue, *things change*. The pacing changes. The rhythm, even the tone, can change. The way the page looks is different. And in trying to strengthen the chapter the day before, you might have made *new problems* you didn't realize, both big and small. Coming to the chapter again a day later is like a second chance, revealing what works from the previous day's work and what might have seemed a good idea at the time but actually weakens the story considerably.

3. It also helps remind you where the previous chapter left off, in terms of pacing, structure, tone, character goals, conflict, etc, when you continue onto the *new* chapter. A day can be a long time, and when you just start straight into the next chapter without re-reading the chapter from the day before,

you might forget elements from the previous scene that now changes bits and pieces to come in the next scene.

In the end, do what's right for you.

Reading chapters twice in each revision essentially makes things easier for you, the writer.

And I find it essential these days, whether I'm working on the first major revision of a book I just recently drafted or I'm working on the tenth draft really far down the line.

Reading your chapters twice allows you two chances instead of one to fix problems, both big and small, and it gives you more opportunities to improve your work.

So give it a try if you've never revised this way in the past!

You might find your revisions going far better than they ever have before.

65. Why Your Novel Needs More Drafts Than You Think

Unless you're a hugely gifted writer, I would suggest that you complete many drafts of your novel.

I would aim for three drafts of your novel before you send it to beta readers to look at and critique your work. I would *never* send out a first draft to anyone. First drafts are terrible. There are sentences that don't make sense. Typo after typo on every page. Character motivations that seem to switch every other chapter.

At minimum you should do two drafts before anyone else reads your work. Three drafts? Even better. Three drafts allows you the time to not perfect your work necessarily but make it fully presentable to others.

How many drafts should you complete before you start querying literary agents?

Again, at least three. For the love of God, at least three!

But this is another case where a couple more drafts will do you good. It's better to take another month or two to complete additional drafts than to query agents with a manuscript that's only 80% there.

Why waste six months of your life on a book that gets only rejections from agents when you could spend eight months, maybe ten, getting your book exactly where it needs to be?

I have at least five unpublished manuscripts in the drawer that might have received more interest from agents if I had just spent a *few more weeks* working on them, getting more feedback from friends and writers I admire and trust.

Don't do what I've done in the past. Take your manuscripts to the finish line no matter how long it takes.

Here's a schedule you might try to follow when it comes to writing and revising your novel...

1. Write the first draft. Write it fast. Aim for 2,000 words a day if possible. Or 1,000 if that's more manageable. Even 500 words a day is solid.

2. When you finish the first draft, put the novel in a drawer *for at least four weeks*, if not six weeks or longer. Let the book rest for a bit.

3. Then do a second draft all on your own. This often takes me three to four weeks to go through every chapter, fixing things I see along the way and cutting a lot of fluff as I *also* take notes on the side for things I want to improve in the third draft.

4. Take another break from the manuscript. Four weeks minimum.

5. Now do a third draft all on your own and incorporate most of the notes you wrote down as you read through the second draft. By the end of this third draft, you will *finally* have a manuscript closer to how you envisioned your story when you first began writing it.

6. Now find three to five people to beta read your third draft. Give them at least four weeks to read the novel and get back to you with their thoughts. I have had close friends read my work, and I have also had more casual writer friends take a look. I put out a call in 2018 for beta readers for my MFA thesis novel, and I had *fifteen people* agree to take a look at it! Fifteen, which I eventually whittled down to seven.

7. Your fourth draft should bring into account the feedback from your beta readers. If all five of them don't like something about your manuscript, *you need to do something about that problem*. If only one of them criticizes something you love, then maybe it can stay. It's up to you.

8. Once you've finished this draft, you might be ready to start querying your book to literary agents.

Complete a few drafts of your query letter during this time. Research all the agents. Put together a database of who you plan to send it to. And don't forget to write a two-page synopsis of your novel as well.

9. But before you query, yes, go through your novel *one last time.* You shouldn't be changing much story-wise in the fifth draft. This draft is for locating typos, awkward sentences, misspellings, things like that. In this fifth draft, make your work *as clean and polished as possible.* When you finish, I would go back and re-read your first ten pages one last time too, just because many agents ask to see the opening pages of your novel, and you want those to shine their brightest.

10. Okay. Take a breath. It's been seven or eight months since you wrote the first word of your book, maybe longer. I know it's been hard, and it's taken forever. But it's finally time, I promise. Now you can start querying your novel to agents!

This is by no means the only way to write and revise a novel.

You might have a different process of your own that works better. At the end of the day, just remember this: revision is key if you want to be a successful writer. Do not ignore the revising process. And don't just do a second draft and think your work is perfect and ready.

Take revision seriously, and you will go far, I guarantee it!

66. Why You Need to Consider the Lengths of Your Paragraphs

I think a lot about the lengths of the paragraphs in my writing.

I think about the way my paragraphs look on any given page of my latest novel.

Something I've learned from many fantastic authors is how to vary the lengths of my paragraphs to create a rhythm for my writing that works exceedingly well for the reader.

Write huge block paragraphs over and over, and you'll bog down your reader.

No matter how beautiful your writing is, no matter how perfectly chosen the words, a massive paragraph on any given page in your novel will turn off and intimidate many readers.

Write lots of little sentence-long paragraphs over and over, however, and you won't give your readers enough meat in terms of action, description, character.

If every paragraph is one or two sentences, the rhythm becomes almost too fast at times and your reader will likely start flipping through the pages at an accelerated rate, skipping over moments you as the author might deem to be important.

The trick is to have a healthy mix of the shorter paragraphs and the longer paragraphs.

You really do need a healthy mix no matter what genre or age market you're writing toward.

It would make sense to write shorter paragraphs throughout most of my work since I primarily write for the middle grade and young adult markets, right?

Yes, it's true… to an extent. In my newest young adult novel, for example, I integrate a lot of shorter paragraphs, plenty of dialogue, moments that only have the occasional bits of description.

But I also trust in my young adult reader to stick around when I include the occasionally long paragraph or moment of heavy description. I do believe readers young and old will stick with you through some longer paragraphs as long as they're engaged with the story and characters.

The majority of the time though, even in fiction written for older readers, it is in your best interest to keep your longer paragraphs to a minimum.

And when you do include a longer paragraph, make sure there's an excellent reason for it. Make sure it works with the rhythm of your storytelling and look closely at every sentence to ensure it needs to be there.

I typically will look at the way my paragraphs look from one revision to the next. And you should, too.

If I feel like there is too much in the way of shorter sentences, where, say, five pages in a row is just dialogue and one-to-two-sentence paragraphs, I'll think about maybe taking one of those short paragraphs and expanding it a little or maybe writing a new paragraph from scratch.

Now, keep this in mind: don't obsess over your paragraph lengths when you write *the first draft.*

Just keep the idea in the back of your mind that you should include lots of shorter paragraphs and the occasional longer paragraph. Have a balance. Don't go too far one way or the other.

And then when you're revising I would advise you do a draft where you specifically examine how your paragraphs look on the page

If you find yourself seeing too many pages in a row with lots of huge paragraphs or lots of white space and brief one-sentence paragraphs, ask yourself if you can vary up your paragraph length.

You can do this by adding a single new paragraph, building onto an existing one, or cutting down on what you already have.

Paragraphs make a story. Make sure you're using the best ones you can!

67. Why You Need to Remove Adverbs from Your Fiction Writing

Oh, the dreaded adverb.

Every time I write an adverb, especially in the first draft of a long manuscript, I wince, and I want to cut it, I *desperately* want to remove it then and there, but my practice in writing a first draft is to always keep going, don't slow down to edit, always focus on the next paragraph, the next sentence.

And then there's the second draft, when I also catch hundreds of adverbs and don't delete enough of them.

It's usually not until the fifth or sixth draft, when I'm doing more line level editing, that I will take a few days and do the best I can to cut out as many adverbs as I can find.

Because the truth of the matter is that adverbs *weaken your writing*.

They slow the pacing of a sentence. They usually tell the reader something rather than show it. They usually read awkwardly (see what I mean?).

I would suggest that 95% of the time, you can *always* find a better way to describe an action than with an adverb.

Which ones fire off my fingertips the most? Slowly and quickly.

I can't tell you how many times in a first draft of a novel or a short story I use the words *slowly* and *quickly*.

They're the easy go-to adverbs. I want the reader to understand my protagonist is moving especially slow through the woods, and so I write, "He walks slowly down the path."

There. Done, right? I'm a literary genius. The Pulitzer is mine!

The problem is that this sentence sucks. There's nothing original about it. Nothing interesting or flashy. It's a sentence that equals death in the imagination of the reader.

The main character is walking at a slow pace down the path. Okay, what about, "He walks with trepidation down the path."

Better, right? Still not great, because, again, you're telling the reader something here. It's always better, whenever possible, to *show* the reader. So try this instead:

"He tiptoes down the path, sweat dripping off his cheeks and chin, his arms trembling even though the air is warm and the sun is bright."

Again, not the best sentence in the history of the world, but you can see how that's better than "He walks slowly down the path." It's monumentally better.

Now, I'm not advising you eliminate every single adverb in your manuscript.

You're going to have the occasional sentence that an adverb works fine for, but I would suggest for every ten uses, eliminate nine of them if you can. Adverbs are not your friends. Don't treat them as such.

Of course there are thousands of different kinds of adverbs. He shut the door *firmly*. She dropped to the ground *restfully*. They argued their points *maniacally*.

If you want to win the Worst Writer of the Year award, you can go ahead and put an adverb in pretty much any sentence you want!

But no, please don't do this. It's so easy to be rejected as a writer. So easy for others to tell you *no*.

You want to do everything in your power to get them to say yes, and too many adverbs will bring your writing down.

Again, you don't have to cut out *all* of them. But if you want to make your latest manuscript soar, I would advise you spend a few days and look for those sometimes hard-to-find adverbs.

This practice will make you a better writer, I guarantee it!

68. Why You Need to Avoid Clichés in Your Writing

Clichés in writing often happen accidentally.

You don't sit down to do your writing that day necessarily *meaning* to write a cliché or two. Or three. Or ten.

You're trying to find the best way to write a sentence, something comes to mind, and you type the words. The sentence sounds good, so you move on.

Here's the deal: you're going to write clichés in a first draft.

They're going to be everywhere on a micro level, and you might even have some at a macro level.

The trick is to find them when you revise your work, and eliminate as many as you can, hopefully all of them.

Clichés come in many forms, shapes, and sizes, like the following…

The Micro Level

When you write a really strong simile or metaphor that works and is unique, your writing soars, and your reader will likely crack a smile.

When the similes and metaphors are clichés, however, your reader will probably groan.

You know the typical ones: *happy as a clam, light as a feather, pretty as a picture.*

Worse, there are the even more obvious clichés we see and hear practically on a daily basis: *the rest is history, every cloud has a silver lining, don't judge a book by its cover.*

Your writing should have none of these. These kind of similes and images might fly off your fingertips when you're powering through the latest pages of your first draft, but keeping them there in your revisions is a big no-no. These kinds of phrases stink like you know what. Avoid!

The Macro Level

You should also look at any clichés you're dealing with at a macro level in your fiction writing.

Think of the premise of your novel before you write it. Think of the backstory you've created for your main character. Is anything obvious?

Is anything something we've all read before in other books or seen before in a dozen movies?

You can get away with clichés here and there in a novel, I suppose, since there's so many words you're working with, but you should at least try to avoid clichés when it comes to the major elements of your story. The first draft of a novel takes months to write. After that, you'll spend a few more months, possibly years revising it.

Always work on novels that you're passionate about, that you feel absolutely compelled to write, and, yes, that are free of clichés.

You want to write a novel that is wholly unique and something only *you* could write. Don't waste months or years writing a book that has a clichéd concept, or one-note, clichéd characters.

Find that idea that is original, that excites you to no end.

And avoid clichés like the plague! (See what I did there?)

69. Why It's Important to Kill Your Darlings

Kill your darlings.

You've heard it before, I'm sure. William Faulkner is famous for saying it.

It's that phrase we writers often try to ignore.

We often think that it's one geared toward *other* writers, those *other* creative types that don't know what they're doing.

Certainly I will never have to kill my darlings, right? *Right?*

Sad to say, yes you will. You cannot be precious with your writing. If you do, your writing may suffer for it.

Let's look at three different levels of killing your darlings—the micro level (sentence & paragraphs), the first macro level (chapters), and the second macro level (characters)…

1. The Micro Level—Sentences & Paragraphs

Kill your darlings can mean both the big and the small of your manuscript. Sometimes it's as simple as a single sentence, one you feel is brilliant and perfect and should never be removed.

You might go through ten drafts, always making sure that beautiful sentence stays in chapter seven, even though most of chapter seven has changed and now the sentence doesn't make any sense. It doesn't matter, the sentence is staying, you say.

This is an example of why it's important to kill your darlings at the micro level.

Yes, that sentence might be amazing. Yes, it might astound a few of your readers. But if the sentence shouldn't be there any longer for whatever reason, then, yes, it needs to go! Even if it's the best sentence of the chapter, or heck, the entire book.

2. The Macro Level—Chapters

Kill your darlings isn't just for the occasional sentence though. It can be geared toward much bigger elements of your manuscript, and in just the past two years I've seen it all.

Let's go with a super big one next. This one might sting; it certainly did for me. You might have to not only cut that precious sentence; you might have to cut that precious *chapter* you love so much, too. Even worse, you might have to cut a whole *bunch* of chapters, like I've had to do in multiple novels in the past. On my MFA thesis novel I had to cut *seven chapters* in the second draft, which was super painful.

More than two years later I still think about those lost chapters. There was some great writing in those scenes, a few heart-stopping moments that would have shocked and pleased a lot of readers.

But at the end of the day, that section didn't belong in the book, and all these months later, the book is so much better without those chapters.

It needed to go. And so I'm happy I learned earlier in the revising process what I had to do.

It might be hard for you to see what chapters belong and which don't all on your own. This is why it's important after your second or third draft to find beta readers, people to look at your work and give you feedback.

You might not have a thesis adviser to comb through your writing like I did, but you can always find awesome beta readers to tell you the news you sometimes don't want to hear. Use them!

3. The Macro Level—Characters

So yes, sometimes you have to kill your darling sentences, and sometimes you have to kill some darling paragraphs, and pages, and chapters.

But you know what hurts the most? What's so painful I actually wrote a short story about it? When kill your darlings refers to killing off one or more of your *characters*.

This doesn't mean literally killing the characters in the narrative of your manuscript. No, this means removing them from your manuscript completely as if they never existed. Characters who played a major role in a previous draft, now gone in the next draft, never to be seen again.

This happened on my newest middle grade novel. In the first two drafts, there were two male supporting characters that were sprinkled throughout the narrative who played huge parts in the third act, especially in the hair-raising finale.

But later I decided that in order to make the manuscript stronger and tighter, those two male characters had to go.

And even though removing them ultimately made for a better book, it was hard.

It's really, really hard to give life to two people on the page, only to rip them out of the manuscript forever. It hurts *every single time*.

That's why they call it kill your darlings.

You the writer might find parts of your novel to be precious, anything from a sentence to chapters and characters.

But no matter how far along you are in the process, you need to do what's best for the story. You need to think about what you set out to do in the first place and try to accomplish that through your revision process however necessary.

Even if you have to add and delete big sections of the book. Even if you have to cut a character or two or three.

Kill your darlings now, and your manuscript will soar later.

Kill your darlings now, and your writing will only get better!

70. Why You Should Never Have to Explain Your Fiction to Readers

You should never have to explain elements of your story to your readers.

When it comes to critiques you receive about your novel, you might as the author feel the need to explain, explain, explain—especially when people begin discussing an element of your work that confuses them.

Whether you're a part of a workshop, or if you're just talking to a person who read your latest work and wants to give you feedback, you the writer will always want to explain things that for whatever reason didn't make sense. You will want to make it clear that the writing isn't the problem, it's the person who didn't read your writing close enough.

Now sure, it's possible that something you wrote will make sense for 99.9% of your readers, and that it *just so happens* one particular person didn't pick up on something.

But there's about a 0.01% chance that's the case, sorry to say. Especially when two or more people don't understand something about your story.

If a part of your story doesn't make sense to readers, don't explain. Instead, do another revision.

This is why beta readers are so important. This is why you have to have people look at your work before you start sending it out to literary agents and editors.

You can discover what a group of people don't understand in your latest work of fiction and then you can figure out what you need to do next to improve upon it.

Again, don't feel the need to explain to the readers what they don't understand. The explanation might be a good one, and it often is! Twenty seconds of explanation, and many readers will say, *ohhhh, okay, I get it now, thanks for that!*

But this isn't good enough. You know why?

If your story or novel gets published, you can't always be there to give an explanation!

Your novel gets published, and when a reader sits down to read your book, *you're not there.* You're not around to whisper explanations into your reader's ear… so you better make sure your writing makes sense.

This is why revision is so important. This is why I always tell other writers not to stop at draft two or three but to push yourself to draft five or six, possibly more. To get your novel to the best possible place.

You don't really have an excuse to only take your fiction 85% of the way. My feeling is that if you're going to spend months and months on a project, why not do everything you can to make sure it's 100% what you want it to be?

So ignore the desire to explain. Let your writing, always, speak for itself. And if it doesn't?

Then it's time for the next draft.

71. Why Beta Readers are So Important to Your Success as a Writer

First of all, what is a beta reader?

A beta reader is essentially a non-professional who will read your manuscript before you query or publish the book and give you helpful feedback. These people offer their valuable time to help you get better. A beta reader is usually unpaid and not someone, like an editor, who is often compensated for their work.

Another important thing about a beta reader? They are absolutely critical to your success as a writer.

I didn't believe this for the longest time. I rarely considered using beta readers. I thought I could do it on my own. I could revise my books without help from anybody. I knew my story, my characters, my world. What was a beta reader going to tell me that would possibly make my novel better?

I plugged along for many years writing novel after novel… and finding no success. I figured I just hadn't written the right story yet, and that in due time my success would come.

Looking back I wish I had started looking for beta readers so much sooner.

In fact, I wish I'd had beta readers—even just one or two of them—from the very beginning.

Because here's the thing—beta readers aren't out to get you. They don't want to hate on your book and tell you the fifty-six reasons why it's terrible.

Yes, there will be negative feedback. Yes, there will be constructive criticism. Any beta reader worth a damn is going to tell you things about your book that aren't working and that need to be changed.

And yes, hearing some of this will be hard. It *still* is hard for me to hear it sometimes.

But it's simply part of the process. Finding beta readers is something I urge you to do because this one step might mean the difference of your book being sold to a publisher or being put into your office drawer for all eternity.

I started using beta readers a few years back.

When it came to a young adult novel I wrote in 2015, I decided I wanted to do two things before I sent out the query letter. First, I wanted at least three beta readers to read the novel and give me notes, and second, I wanted at least one person to read and critique my query letter as well.

The novel ended up not being signed by a literary agent (and yes, it's still sitting in my office drawer), but the book had its full manuscript requested from *twenty agents* over the course of a year, an all-time record for me. And that's something I'll never forget.

In 2018 I put out a call for beta readers for my MFA thesis novel, and *fifteen people* said they would read it for me and give me feedback. I decided that was too extreme, so I picked five of them—a mix of friends and MFA colleagues—to read the book and give me notes.

This part of the process took about ten long weeks, but it was an essential step in making the manuscript better.

Beta readers are ultimately important to your writing career for three key reasons.

One, taking the time to let your manuscript rest while beta readers take a look at it and prepare you feedback is good for you to step away from the project and put your mind elsewhere.

When you read through the feedback of your beta readers, you won't want to challenge every critical thing they say and you won't throw their feedback in the trash and say they're wrong. Once you've taken a break from your book, you'll actually enjoy their feedback and look toward ways to make your manuscript better!

Two, beta readers will notice things about your novel you never would have thought of in a million years. This certainly happened on my MFA thesis novel. Two of my beta readers in particular found flaws in my characters and storyline that were absolutely on the money and not things I would have thought about as I continued revising the project.

Three, beta readers will be your first fans in a way, people who you know and who you trust who will talk up your books to others as you continue revising the project and ultimately querying it to agents. Unless the beta readers absolutely hate your book (which rarely happens), you will have your first fans of your work in the world, people who have read an early version and desperately want to see your story published in its finished form.

A few final tips about beta readers…

So how do you find beta readers if you have no idea where to look? Try online writing communities, on Facebook and Twitter. Those have worked well for me. Also think about people you know and who you've interacted with. Think about joining an in-person writing group, or pursue an MFA in Creative Writing, like I did.

And keep this in mind, too, when it comes to beta readers: you shouldn't implement into your latest draft *every single note they provided*. Don't go through the next draft fixing and changing every little thing they put down in your feedback letter. Use the notes that make sense to you, that feel right, and feel free to disregard the ones that don't.

It will be hard to read the negative criticism. You will want to disregard all of it at first.

But remember this: if one of your beta readers criticizes something about your novel you intensely disagree with, then you can move on, but if *all* of your beta readers criticize the same thing, then you absolutely need to address that issue in your next revision!

In the end, remember that beta readers are out there to help you, not hurt you. They want to help make your writing career a success.

You can't do this alone, I'm telling you. You need honest, intelligent, thoughtful beta readers to look at your work from time and time and give you the feedback you need to make your novel the best it can be.

72. 10 Words to Look For When You're Editing Your Writing

There's a lot to think about when you're editing your own work.

Whether it's your fifth revision or your fifteenth, you're always hard at work on making your book better. You want your characters to come more alive, you want the story to make sense, you want the writing to have strong pacing, you want to write something *spectacular*!

When you're in the early revising stages, you should pay attention to larger story issues, not words and sentences. Before you get to the smaller details, you want to make sure the story works as best as it can.

But later on, once your story is solid and your characters are as rich and complex as you can make them, *then* you should start paying attention to the specific words that make up your story.

As I slowly make my way through my novel manuscripts chapter by chapter, these are ten words I'm always looking for to be changed or deleted. And you know what? You should be looking for these words, too!

1. That

My MFA thesis advisor taught me a lot when I worked with her on improving my writing, but you know what one of the greatest things she taught me was?

The word "that" can often be removed from your writing. The word "that" is often an unnecessary placeholder!

I started looking for "that" in my fiction and soon realized she was right. About 90% of the time, "that" can be removed from a sentence without changing anything about the sentence itself. I had written it into so many sentences for twenty years, and it rarely needed to be there, holy cow!

Example: ***She walked faster so that she could arrive at the party on time.***

The sentence is perfectly fine, but what happens when you remove "that" from it? Nothing. The sentence stays the same, and it sounds better.

2. Just

This word will be the death of me. I use it *all the time*. I often use it three to five times on every single page of my fiction writing without realizing it.

My MA thesis advisor (yes, I have both an MA in English and an MFA in Creative Writing!) was the first person to teach me how the word "just" should always go. He didn't say almost always. He said *always*.

Even today I have to push back on that a little bit. I do think occasionally the word "just" helps a sentence. Not only with the pacing of it but also to tell the reader something about time and place.

But I agree that 95% of the time, you should remove "just" from your writing. You'll be shocked to see how much your work strengthens in time.

Example: ***She just left to arrive at the party on time.***

Here's a case of a sentence where "just" is definitely not needed. Take it out, and the sentence stays basically the same. Now if a character says this line in dialogue? Then the "just" can stay possibly. But otherwise, take it out.

3. Start/Begin

This one a writer friend pointed out to me once. I'd never put much thought into it, but it makes sense. And I didn't realize how much I was using this one, too.

So often in my fiction I'll write "she began to walk to her car" instead of "she walked to her car." I'll say "she started to walk to her," too, if I already used "began" earlier on the page. I go back and forth between those two goddamn words like it's nobody's business.

As you're editing your novel you should go through your sentences and search out every "start" and "begin." Try to cut 90% or more of them, and your writing will improve considerably.

Example: ***She began to walk to her car to get to the party on time.***

Ugh, am I right? It sounds incredibly awkward. Why is she beginning to walk to her car? Why can't she walk to her car without a beginning or ending? Remove "began to" to make the sentence sound better for the reader.

4. Really/Very

My high school journalism teacher pulled me aside once to tell me to stop using the word "very" in my writing. He said the word meant nothing.

This confused me at the time. I didn't understand how it could mean nothing. It meant extra. It meant extremely. How dare he hate so much on the word, honestly!

But, of course, the man was right. The words "very" and "really" don't add anything to your sentences. They're placeholders for something better.

Again, if a character says "very" or "really" in a line of dialogue, then fine. But if you're describing something in your fiction, or if you're trying to express a feeling from one of the characters, ask yourself if you need "very" or "really." What do these words add? Like my journalism teacher said, they add nothing.

Example: ***She walked to her car really fast to get to the party on time.***

This sentence isn't a great one to begin with, but it gets a whole lot better when you eliminate "really." Fast is fast. Really fast doesn't give the reader any kind of unique image. Find something else to make the sentence stand out. How does she walk fast? Add more description.

5. Immediately

This is a word nobody specifically has taught me to remove from my fiction, but I found it three times in a chapter of one of my recent novels, and a lightbulb went off in my head that maybe I should *keep* looking for it. Lo and behold it's popped up at least once in almost every chapter since.

This word doesn't add anything to the sentence. Sure, it seems like it might add a level of urgency, but it doesn't. It's long and ugly and brings nothing of note to any of your sentences.

Example: ***She immediately walked to her car to get to the party on time.***

Okay, so this tells me she walked to her car right away instead of, what, five or ten seconds from now? Again, it's lazy. It doesn't give the reader an image. It's yet another placeholder for something else.

6. Then

This is a word I use all the time in my writing, and I have no idea why. What does the word "then" really do for a sentence? How does it add anything?

My thinking sometimes is I've used "and" too much in the previous sentences, so I want to add a "then" to differentiate this sentence from the other ones. I feel sometimes it adds better pacing to a sentence, too.

But about 99% of the time, "then" is unnecessary. Here's what you should do—take "then" out of the sentence and see if the meaning of the sentence changes at all. If it doesn't, the word needs to go!

Example: ***She walked fast toward her car and then got inside of it.***

The truth is you don't even need that second part of the sentence. You could cut straight from your character walking to your character driving away.

But notice how "then" adds nothing there. If the sentence ended with "and got inside of it" you and your readers would understand its meaning, right?

Not every use of "then" needs to be cut from your manuscript but cutting most of them will improve your writing considerably.

7. Absolutely / Completely / Totally

I use words like these to make a *very crucial point* oftentimes in my writing. The word I use the most by far is "absolutely." I write it a lot in first drafts. I feel it gives emphasis. And like with "then," it helps with pacing issues.

Sometimes a sentence feels too bare and adding "absolutely" or "completely" does add something to the rhythm.

But here's the problem—words like these three are empty and unnecessary. They're like "very" and "really" in that they don't emphasize much of anything.

Example: **She just left so she could absolutely get to the party on time.**

You might think adding "absolutely" there tells your reader how important it is for your character to arrive at the party on time, but all it does is make the sentence more awkward. It doesn't tell your reader much of anything.

Now, as I've said before, words like these are perfectly fine if they pop up in *dialogue* from time to time, but outside of dialogue, be wary of them.

8. Actually / Probably

Similar to the previous examples, words like "actually" and even "probably" are empty words in your writing. Same goes for words like "certainly" or "virtually" or "basically." They clutter up your sentences and give your readers nothing in return.

The best of the lot is "probably" because it tells the reader *something*, at least. The word "probably" means something might not happen but will in all likelihood.

Something like "actually" though, while serviceable in dialogue, brings nothing of interest to the rest of your writing.

Example: ***She actually ran to her car fast so she could get to the party on time.***

What does "actually" add there? I guess the previous sentence could be someone assuming this female character is slow all the time, but even then, everything your characters do in your fiction is *actually happening*, so how does "actually" serve a purpose?

You should think critically about including any words in your fiction that ends in -ly. Many of them can be deleted or changed, and that's the case with the words above.

9. Rather / Quite

Here are two more words that might be even emptier than words like "absolutely" and "actually." My journalism teacher once told me I was using the word "quite" too much and I needed to strike most examples of it from my writing. I didn't understand at the time what was so wrong with "quite." What did that damn word ever do to my journalism teacher?

But Mr. Halcomb was right. Words like "quite" and "rather" are empty words only added to sentences for rhythm and pacing purposes. Sometimes a sentence sounds better with one or the other there, even though neither word adds anything of value.

Example: ***She walked to her car quite fast to get to the party on time.***

In this example, "quite" serves as a placeholder for some aforementioned words like "really" or "very" or "totally." It's another shrug of a word you see in writing all the time and wonder to yourself, *why?*

Did she walk to her car fast? Or did she walk to it quite fast? Is there a difference? Nope! And when there's no difference, the word needs to go.

10. Any Dialogue Tag Besides Said or Asked

Finally, we come to dialogue tags. I use them in my fiction all the time. "He said" and "she asked" help do two things—tell your reader who is speaking and help with the rhythm of the scene. You don't want your dialogue to go back and forth forever without an occasional dialogue tag to break things up.

But at the same time you want your dialogue tags to be invisible. You don't want them to stand out in a negative way to your reader.

How do tags stand out in a negative way? When you use something other than "said" or "asked."

Example: ***"I need to get to my car so I can arrive at the party on time!" she begged.***

What else could she do here? She could "exclaim" the line or "threaten" the line or "scream" the line or "cough" the line or a hundred other hilarious examples you can come up with.

Having her "beg" that line of dialogue gives the reader more info about how she's saying the line, sure, but begging a line of dialogue doesn't make much sense, and plus, putting "beg" there won't fully register for your reader if they're already invested in the scene and the characters.

So please—use only "said" or "asked" in your dialogue tags. Doing so is a mark of a professional writer always!

There are plenty more words you might want to look for when you're editing but start with these.

Your writing will soar when you change or delete specific words like these ones.

You might not think it's so when you're slowly working through your manuscript sentence by sentence. You might think to yourself, *nobody's going to pay attention to specific words, are they?*

The truth is they will, especially those gatekeepers who have the power to say yes to your work and get it published. You don't want to give them any reasons to say no. You want your writing to be its very best.

So every time you edit your manuscript, look for these words, and try to delete most of them if you can. Trust me—you'll be glad you did!

73. 10 Phrases to Look For When You're Editing Your Writing

We looked at ten specific words you should look for when you're editing your work. Now let's discuss ten painful *phrases* you should always be looking for as well…

1. For a few seconds / for a moment

I write phrases like these two all the time in a first draft in a work of fiction. They're all over the place. Sometimes they pop up more than once on the same page!

The big problem with phrases like these is that they don't mean much to your readers. Seriously, what does "for a moment" even mean? It tells the reader the character is taking a beat, but this isn't a movie. How much time that moment lasts isn't exactly clear to the reader.

Writing "for a few seconds" or "for a moment" is lazy ultimately because you should instead be writing something more unique and dynamic to demonstrate that your character is taking a necessary beat.

Example: ***He stared at her for a few seconds, scratching the bottom of his chin.***

This whole sentence is lazy, honestly, but it's made even worse with "for a few seconds." What happens to the sentence when you take that phrase out? Nothing. The meaning comes across exactly the same. It's clear a beat is being taken, so why add "for a few seconds?"

There might be one or two places in a work of fiction where "for a moment" or something similar can stay, but for the most part, stay clear of phrases like these always.

2. She knows / thinks / hopes / wonders / feels / believes

Did you know your writing improves considerably when you remove sentences that have words like "knows" and "thinks" and "hopes" and "wonders" and "feels" and "believes?"

Why? Because it's *telling*, not showing.

A few years ago I learned writing gets infinitely better when you stay away from merely telling the reader things about your character. Sentences that begin with a character thinking something or hoping something or feeling something. *Especially* feeling.

Any schmuck can write a sentence like the following…

Example: **She felt embarrassed by the incident in the cafeteria yesterday.**

Again, this is lazy writing. It's an author telling the reader something rather than showing it in an interesting way.

Don't simply tell us she's embarrassed about something that happened yesterday. *Show* us in her behavior and mannerisms how she's embarrassed by it.

Same thing goes for a character hoping for something or wondering what might happen next. Show us this, don't tell us.

3. For the most part / after all / at the end of the day

I go nuts with phrases like these in my writing. Often I find that these phrases help with the rhythm of my sentences and paragraphs. But there's one big problem with phrases like "for the most part" and "at the end of the day."

They're empty. They mean nothing. And they don't need to be there.

Example: **She turned away from Billy. She had no more desire to see him, after all. Their friendship was over.**

See how the sentence doesn't really change if you drop "after all?" It can be dropped because it's empty. It's there for rhythm, nothing else.

Whenever you're stuck deciding whether or not a phrase needs to go, ask yourself this: does the meaning of the sentence stay the same if I cut the phrase?

In the cases of these three phrases, the answer is almost always a hard yes.

4. There was / it was

My MA thesis advisor was the first person to teach me why sentences that begin with either of these phrases should be rewritten. Like the previous example, "there was" and "it was" can often be empty.

If "it" refers to a subject from the previous sentence, that might be okay, but when you write a sentence like the following, you're in trouble.

Example: ***It was the middle of the night, and Jimmy was still awake.***

What does the "it" refer to in that sentence? Nothing. It's empty.

Now, as my MA thesis advisor did also say, sometimes you have to open a sentence with "there was" or "it was" when referring to the time of day. Occasionally there's not another way to say "it was 10:30 P.M." that to say "it was 10:30 P.M."

But whenever possible, try not to open a sentence with "there was" or "it was." Open sentences with those phrases as seldomly as possible, and your writing will improve in the long run.

5. She nods / shrugs / smiles / grins

Phrases like these are fine, they're *acceptable*, I certainly write them in my fiction from time to time.

But it will serve you well to search for phrases like these in your work and delete some of them and punch up a few others.

Again, any schmuck can write "She nods" before a line of dialogue. It's so basic and boring. So empty.

Example: **She shrugged, then turned her head toward Tiffany and smiled.**

Ugh, am I right? That sentence reeks of amateur hour. What other behavior might you come up with? What's something more unique to the character?

Sure, sometimes for rhythm, you can get away with an occasional "he grins" or "she nods" but try to be better. Try to come up with behavior that enlivens the scene, that develops the character, that shows in more detail the character's emotions.

6. The fact that

Here's a phrase people use in real life all the time. And if you have a character who says it in your story here and there, then that's probably fine.

The problem with a phrase like this is that it's meaningless and wordy. You can usually shorten it to something simpler.

Example: **He would have been faster getting to his car except for the fact that he was talking on the phone.**

Ugh, am I right? It's *so* wordy and awkward. What happens when you remove "for the fact that?" Nothing.

The sentence is shorter and clearer. And the idea stays the same.

Whenever you're in doubt, take the phrase out. And see if anything changes. If it doesn't, it needs to go.

7. In order to

I've been catching this phrase a lot in my latest young adult novel I'm currently editing. It's certainly not as empty as "the fact that." There's a bit more meaning to this particular phrase.

It's still worth changing, however, because it's often unnecessary, and it can often stink up an otherwise decent sentence.

Example: **He walked fast to his car in order to arrive at the party on time.**

Yes, we understand what this sentence is telling us, but is there a way to shorten it? What if you remove "in order" and keep the rest of the sentence the same?

Well, look at that, it stays *exactly the same*. And the rhythm of the sentences improves, too. I'm not sure if there's ever going to be a case where you need "in order to" rather than just "to." Something to think about.

8. Whether or not

Here's another one I use often. I've been saying this phrase for so long in my own life oftentimes it creeps into my fiction writing, and I have to seek it out in the editing stage.

The first word of the phrase is usually fine. The sentence usually doesn't make sense without the "whether" part. But do you need "or not" as well?

Example: ***He wasn't sure whether or not he would arrive to the party on time.***

You read a sentence like that, and, as in the case of the previous examples, it makes perfect sense, but it can still be improved. It can be shortened and say the exact same thing.

Cut "or not" out of there and what do you get? A much better sentence!

9. In terms of

Here's a phrase that will get you a few extra words in your manuscript if they're needed, but, like with our other examples above, it doesn't add up to much.

What is this phrase really saying? Nothing. It's meaningless. It's pointless. And it won't make your readers happy.

Example: ***In terms of how slow he was walking, he wasn't sure if he'd make it to the party on time.***

Oh, man, what a godawful sentence. I've probably written a few sentences like that one before, and I sure hope I fixed them later!

Change a sentence like this one to "He was walking slowly and wasn't sure if…" and you have a better, if still not great, sentence. Make each sentence of yours clear and direct and try not to dress it up with awkward phrases like this one.

10. All of the

Finally, here's something that took me well into my graduate school days to learn: in phrases like this one you don't need the "of."

But we still add it in our lives and on the page, even when you don't need to.

Example: ***He walked with all of the strength he could muster to get to the party on time.***

Again, not a great sentence, but it's made a little better with the elimination of a single word: "of." He doesn't need to walk with all of the strength. He can walk with *all the* strength. "Of" doesn't add anything there. It makes for wordiness, pure and simple.

Sometimes you don't need "all" either, remember that. Sometimes you can get your point across with even fewer words in the long run.

Avoid phrases like these in your writing, and your work will strengthen considerably.

As I said before, it's perfectly fine to include examples of these phrases in your first draft, even your second or third draft. In the beginning you want to focus on *telling your story* the best you can. Get the story right first. Focus on character development and theme and pacing.

But later in the process you want to seek out empty and awkward phrases like these above examples. What makes it so easy is that all you have to do is type any one of these phrases in the search function on Microsoft Word and every example of the phrase will pop up in your manuscript in seconds.

If you have ten examples of "for a moment" or "after all" or "he nods," you can find them quickly and fix, delete, or change as many of them as you can!

74. 5 Words You Should Add Variety To When You're Editing

———

There's a lot you need to keep in mind when you're editing your work.

You want to make sure your writing flows, that the pacing is strong, that your paragraphs and sentences make perfect sense for the reader.

Yes, your storytelling and your characters come first, always, but once your work is at a level you're happy with, it's important to take a few more passes at your manuscript to make it even *a little bit better.*

Changing or deleting specific words and phrases will improve your writing tremendously. You know what else will help, too? Adding *variety* to the words you use often.

I just finished one last draft of my newest short story, and part of the editing work I did this time was locate specific words I use often in my writing and give them some variety so I wasn't ever using the same kind of word over and over from the first page to the last.

What are those words I use often, and that you might use often, too? Let's discuss…

1. Look

Here's a word I use more than almost any other. All right, maybe not more than "the" and "a" and "it," but you know what I'm saying. My characters look at each other *so much of the time.* They're always looking. And in some ways this is a word I've come to despise because I see it so often in my work.

There are two strategies I take when it comes to the word "look." I first search for the word from the beginning of my manuscript to the end and see if there's any uses of it I can delete completely. Often half or more I can cut.

But sometimes you need to explain to the reader what the character is looking at, so it needs to stay. But this doesn't mean you only have to use "look" every time. Try some of these alternatives as well…

- **Peer**—I use this one a lot. It's always an effective alternative that basically means the same thing.
- **Glance**—I use this one if the character is only looking at something or someone for a few seconds.
- **Stare**—And I use this one if the character is looking at something or someone for an obscene amount of time.

And then occasionally I'll use something like "darted his eyes" or "narrowed her eyes" or "averted her gaze," but these always sound awkward to me so I allow myself exactly *one* use of each in anything I write and no more.

2. Sigh

Here's a word I can never get enough of. If I can get through an entire chapter in one of my novels without a single use of this word, I feel like a champion. It's the easy go-to word to break up dialogue or show that a character is feeling something.

Ultimately it's a pretty generic word that doesn't mean a whole lot, so in the case of "sigh," you should avoid it as much as you can. I would say you should only have one use of it in every few chapters when you're writing a novel.

Are there other words you can use for "sigh?" Sure, there are. First, you can rephrase the word so instead of saying "he sighed," you can say "he released a loud, angry sigh," just to give it more detail. But even that isn't great.

Sometimes I'll use these alternatives, too…

- **Groan**—It kind of means the same thing, but it's slightly more agitated.
- **Gasp**—I'll use this word if the character is surprised by something.
- **Exhale**—This one is even more ambiguous than "sigh," but at least it's something different.

I actually didn't realize how often I had my characters sighing until I searched for the word, and trust me, I was *mortified*. So mix this one up as much as you can.

3. Smile

It's hard to admit how often I have my characters smiling, but if they're not sighing at something or looking at somebody, they're most definitely smiling. It's an easy word to use to show that your character is happy about something. You have your character smile, and the reader understands how they're feeling.

The problem with having a character smile too much (and the same goes for having a character cry too often, too) is that the expression gets old for the reader. The character smiles four times in a single chapter, and they start to read like a robot.

You want to mix it up, so here are some other words you can use at times…

- **Grin**—It basically means the same thing, but if you really need to have a character smile twice, on, say, the *same page* of your manuscript, have her smile first and then grin second.

- **Beam**—I use this one only occasionally if the character is really happy, just because the word can read awkward in a context that doesn't make sense.
- **Smirk**—This word is a specific kind of smiling—something that's kind of mocking or condescending—so like with the word "beam," you'll want to use it in the right context.

Like with all of these words, you want to keep "smile" to a minimum if you can. Instead of choosing the easy way by including this basic word, show *why* your character is happy through other details and descriptions whenever possible.

4. Turn

Something else my characters do all the time? They're turning! He turns around here and she turns toward something there, and there's just *so much turning*. Why can't my characters just face forward for once?

The thing is that throughout your story you're going to have characters occasionally turning toward things, there's no way around it. The question then becomes, do you have to use the word "turn" every single time?

Of course not. There are other words that add variety, like these…

- **Move**—This is the obvious one, where instead of writing "he turned around" you can say "he moved the other way" or something simple like that.
- **Spin**—I'm not ashamed to say I use this one sometimes, too, although it does sound a little silly, so I would keep it to a minimum. Saying a character

"spins around" has an almost child-like quality, so I wouldn't use it in a scene of high drama or terror.

- **Twist**—Here's one I also use maybe once or twice in a manuscript, although, like with "spin," it does sound a bit awkward and almost archaic if not used in the right context.

Just keep in mind that you shouldn't only use "turn" over and over again. Some readers might not catch all your uses, but others will.

5. Walk

Here's the final big one. The dreaded word, "walk." Your characters are often coming and going, right? So how else are they usually moving but *walking*?

Of the five words I've gone into, this is the one with the most variety. Let's discuss a few of them…

- **Run**—Here's the easiest alternative to "walk," to show the character is moving fast.
- **Sprint**—Use this one if the character is running really fast.
- **Race**—Sometimes I'll use this if I've used "run" or "sprint" too much in a scene.
- **Amble**—I've always loved this word. It means to "walk casually" basically.
- **Roam**—This one is kind of like "amble" and means "to drift."
- **Saunter**—This one is also kind of similar to "amble" and can be used instead of "stroll."
- **Traipse**—This word is a bit more specific, so I allow myself only one or two uses of it in a manuscript. It means "to walk wearily."

- **Step**—Here's an alternative to "walk" I use often, especially if two characters are standing close to each other and one of the characters moves just a tiny bit closer to the other.

- **Move**—Of course you can on occasion use this word if you've used "walk" too many times in a scene.

- **March**—This one always reads awkwardly to me, so I'll only use it if it makes perfect sense for the context of a scene.

- **Make Her Way**—Also kind of awkward, but you can use it maybe once to mix things up.

- **Perambulate**—OK, that's one's a joke.

On and on and on… you see what I mean. There are ten or more examples I didn't even go into, so, yes, there are lots of ways to say a character walked from place to place.

Although you shouldn't use a new alternative every time, there's simply no excuse to only use "walk" all throughout your manuscript.

Add variety to common words in your writing, and your work will improve every time.

Again, I know it doesn't sound like that big of a deal if you have one too many uses of "look" or "sigh" or "smile" in your writing. If a reader catches two examples of "turn" or "walk" on a single page, that person will probably not even notice, and if they do, they probably *won't care*.

But it absolutely makes you stand out from the crowd if you pay close attention to small details like these and make the effort to take your writing from a nine to a ten, always.

You want to be published, right? You want to find success. Add some variety to the words you include in your writing, and you'll be well on your way!

75. 5 Simple Ways to Trim Down Your Writing

In almost all of your writing, you're eventually going to want to trim it down.

How much varies from case to case, sure, but almost always you reach a certain point in a project where you've said too much and it's in your best interest to cut it back even five to ten percent.

This goes for novels. Short stories. Personal essays. Screenplays. Research papers.

Yes, no matter what kind of writing project you take on, there are five simple ways to trim them down considerably…

1. Delete any sentence that doesn't add substance.

This is the strategy you should start with. If your project is going on too long and you want to shave off some words, a great thing to do is slowly go through it and study each of your sentences. Many of the sentences that can go you'll recognize instantly. Other sentences that can go won't be so obvious on your first read-through, and you might want to go through the manuscript a few more times.

Often there are sentences in your work that don't need to be there. That don't necessarily add any substance. That's telling rather than showing. That repeats something that was already said five pages before.

———

You want all of these to go. You want your piece to be as clean and compelling as possible.

2. Remove all your adverbs.

I know you don't want to. I know you've heard over and over again that adverbs are bad, that *the road to hell is paved with adverbs*, but it's all true. At least 95% of your adverbs should go. Preferably 100% of them. Adverbs weaken your writing, and they often tell your reader things far more often than they show your reader things.

And you know what's great about cutting all or most of your adverbs? You can shave your word count down considerably! You can go through your manuscript page by page and search for all those pesky little "-ly" words that shouldn't be there.

Even in novels, when you have lots more white space to work with, you should cut out most of your adverbs. They rarely serve a purpose.

3. Put extra focus on any block paragraphs.

Block paragraphs aren't much fun to read, am I right? They're often stuffed with long, arduous sentences that should be shaved down. There's usually too much description that goes on and on. You might think your reader needs to know every little thing you add to the paragraph that goes on for a page and a half, but do you *really* need it all?

When you're trying to shave down your word count, a simple strategy to take on is to go through your manuscript page by page and pay particular attention to any paragraph that goes on longer than, say, seven or eight lines. And *certainly* any paragraph that goes on for longer than ten lines.

Read those sentences extra carefully and ask yourself if you need everything. Could you at least shorten some of the sentences? Are there details you could cut by even a few words? A win is getting a fifteen-line paragraph down to twelve lines or ten lines. Or even less!

4. Trim down paragraphs where three or fewer words carry over to the next line.

Here's an excellent trick I picked up a few years back from a screenwriting book, of all things. A screenplay should rarely go over 120 pages, so the authors talked about how if you're at 125 pages or 130 pages, the easiest way to cut the work down is to look for words *carried over* from a previous line and trim enough words to eliminate that extra line.

You can use this strategy in all the writing you do, including novel writing. I use this strategy *all the time*. It's gotten to the point now where I actually get uncomfortable any time I see a single word straggler on its own line.

You'll be shocked at how many words you can cut from your manuscript if you start looking for those stragglers on every page and eliminate all of them.

Depending on the length of your project, it's often hundreds and hundreds of words.

And your manuscript is improved in the process. It's a win-win!

5. Cut every unnecessary word.

This is the last of the strategies you should take on. I'm talking, *the very final read-through* before you start sending out your work.

The last thing you should do is go extra slowly through the manuscript and look for any potential words you can cut. I'm talking every "the" and "at" and "a" or whatever.

Pay close attention to each of your sentences and see if there's a way to trim it down even by a single word.

Give any or all of these five strategies a try in the weeks to come.

They're all fairly simple. There's no big mystery behind any of them, and what's great is if you implement these strategies more and more, they'll come to you naturally.

You'll *automatically* look for sentences that can go, and adverbs, and block paragraphs, and those straggler words carried over from the previous line, and any unnecessary word that shouldn't be there.

You will see *all* of it, and you'll be able to take a writing project that's decent or good… and make it great!

76. Here's One More Easy Way to Improve Your Writing When You're Editing

When you're editing your own writing, there's a lot to look for.

Editing your own work can be tricky. When you're so deep into the world of your story, sometimes it's hard to look at the words and sentences themselves.

But ultimately it's a part of writing you should learn to do well sooner rather than later. Especially if you don't want to find yourself having to pay other editors thousands of dollars to get your work into proper, professional shape.

We've talked about what words and phrases to look for, what words need some variety, and ways to trim your writing down.

But I do believe there's *one more pass* you should take during the editing process that's super easy and not very time-consuming that will make your writing shine its brightest.

You want to remove as many "ing" verbs from your writing as possible.

I didn't learn this until recently, but it's absolutely true. Your writing becomes *so much stronger* when you eliminate most or even all of the "ing" verbs from your manuscript.

Your writing becomes cleaner. It becomes more engaging. Sentences read better. It's something you should start thinking about, for sure.

Let's look at *three examples* and discuss why each sentence is better without the "ing" verb or verbs…

Larry is standing in the middle of the swamp.

Imagine this is the beginning of a novel. You're intrigued why he's in a swamp and also how he could be standing in the center of it. It's not a bad idea to start a work of fiction here.

But look at how the sentence improves just by doing this…

Larry stands in the middle of the swamp.

See how much cleaner that is? You get the same idea across. You maintain the present tense. And you also eliminate a word in the process.

Now let's look at an example with dialogue…

"Go make me dinner," he said, pointing to the oven.

This example might read fine on first glance. Some of your readers might even be okay with it.

But I still think it can be improved by eliminating the "ing" verb.

He pointed to the oven and said, "Go make me dinner."

Sometimes you might think there's no other way for the sentence to work without the "ing" verb, but in almost every case you can find a better way to write the sentence, I'm telling you.

Finally let's look at a more complicated example…

Pulling my chair forward and rolling my eyes, I ask my mother why she's leaving town for so long.

Super awkward, right?

In this example we're going beyond the problem of having "ing" verbs. Now we have verb *modifiers* that tell us something the character is doing before we get to the heart of what the character is *really* doing.

Now, one positive of that above example is that, yes, you can ask your mother that question while pulling your chair forward and rolling your eyes. You can do all three of those things at the same time, so in that regard, the sentence makes logical sense.

Unlike say, "Pulling my chair forward and turning on the television, I start cooking dinner." See how that doesn't make sense? You can't do all three of those things at the same time (unless you have three hands, I suppose!).

Still, that above bolded example isn't great. And it screams of amateur writing.

Look at how the example above improves by doing this…

I pull my chair forward, roll my eyes, and ask my mother why she needs to leave town for so long.

Now I would still change a few things about this example. "Roll my eyes" is a cliché, so I would cut that. And I would probably make that second part of the sentence a line of dialogue.

But again, see how much better that second example is? It's easier to read. It flows well. Your reader will be thankful for a change like this one!

So take a little time to look for "ing" verbs before you send your work into the world.

Okay, okay, you don't have to change *every single one*. You can leave the occasional "ing" verb in a sentence if you truly believe it sounds best that way.

I just looked through my latest novel manuscript, and I have a few "ing" verbs scattered here and there. But instead of having five or ten on any given page, I have one every few pages. Each use of an "ing" verb is so far apart from the previous one and the next one the reader will barely notice them.

What your reader *will* notice, however, is the constant use of "ing" verbs in each paragraph of your writing, especially when you use them as those awkward modifiers like in that example above. You can get away with the occasional "is standing" but using them as modifiers at the

———

beginning of a sentence will bring the level of your writing way, way down.

You want to improve your writing with each new project. And one easy way to do that is to at some point during the editing process eliminate most, if not all, of your "ing" verbs. You'll be glad you did!

All right, you've written your novel, you've revised it and edited it to your heart's content. What's next? Let's talk publishing!

PUBLISHING & COMMUNITY

77. 5 Reasons Why You Need to Sign with a Literary Agent

For many years, signing with a literary agent was always the main goal.

In 2010 I wrote my first novel. I queried it to a few agents, and by the end of the day, an agent requested the full manuscript! The joy I felt that night was like nothing I'd ever experienced before when it came to my writing life, and that joy kept coming in the years that followed whenever I queried a new novel to literary agents and got some requests for pages.

But nothing, absolutely nothing, beats actually signing with an agent, which happened to me in 2017.

When you're an unpublished writer, signing with a literary agent always feels like the beginning of your writing dreams being fulfilled. Signing with an agent means your book *might actually be published*.

Signing with a literary agent should certainly be of interest to you if you are considering traditional publishing for your work, so here are five reasons why you should attempt doing so!

1. A literary agent will make your book better.

Some agents are more editorial than others, but I guarantee you that your agent won't let your book go out on submission to editors until it's ready. Until it's nearly perfect.

If that means just one edit, then consider yourself one of the lucky ones. My novel *Monster Movie* went through *ten* edit rounds before my agent send it out to editors, but you know what? The book needed ten rounds. It needed many, many revisions to be the best book it could be.

2. A literary agent will be there for you during the highs and lows of your writing life.

They'll be there for you for pretty much everything. As someone to bounce ideas off of when you can't decide what novel to write next. As someone to talk to when you're struggling in the latest draft of your book and need some guidance. As someone who will be your number one cheerleader.

A really good literary agent will be there for you, always. And that person will push you to stay focused and creative!

3. A literary agent will have connections in the world of publishing.

This, of course, is one of the big reasons to sign with an agent. There's only so much you can do in your writing career without connections. And without a literary agent, it's nearly impossible to be published by any of the major publishing houses.

A literary agent gives you the opportunity for your work to be considered by editors at these major houses, along with editors at some smaller houses too that only take agented submissions. And they'll get your work to the best editors possible due to their vast connections and knowledge of the industry.

4. A literary agent will help negotiate your contracts.

Remember, literary agents only make money when *you* make money. Any agent who asks for a penny from you for any reason is someone you shouldn't work with, shouldn't trust.

You should find an agent who is ethical and reputable, and who has experience and understanding of the publishing industry when it comes to negotiating contracts. Contracts can be confusing for the writer, and your agent will help you considerably with this part.

5. A literary agent will give your writing career credibility.

Once you sign with a literary agent, you're basically telling the world how serious you are. This isn't some hobby you're doing on the weekend. It's not just a way to pass the time. You're telling the world, *I want to be a published author, I want my stories to find an audience.*

When people ask what you do for a living, you should say you're a writer no matter what, but you should *definitely* say it once you have a literary agent, no matter if you haven't had a book sell yet. It's sometimes hard to feel like a real writer when you haven't been traditionally published, but having a literary agent definitely helps.

Lastly, always remember to do your research.

Not every literary agent is the same. Make sure you do your research, first in agents who represent the kind of writing you do, and second in agents who have sold books in your genre and who will be someone you might like to work with.

If you're thinking of signing with a literary agent in the weeks or months to come, best of luck to you. I hope these tips will help as you continue in your writing journey!

78. 10 Things You Need to Do When Querying Your Novel

It took me awhile to finally sign with a literary agent in 2017. Seven years and sixteen novels, as a matter of fact.

I made a lot of mistakes along the way. And I've certainly learned a lot over the years.

Querying your novel can be terrifying. I know, I've been there. You put your heart and soul into your manuscript for months, possibly years. You've revised and edited the book to your heart's content. You've had a few people beta read it and give you notes.

And now everything you've worked for has come to this: the success or failure of a query letter, a pitch that's short and sweet, that needs to sell your book in a way that convinces a literary agent to request pages.

It can be a daunting task, but it's important, first, that you relax.

And second, that you don't need to make the mistakes I made my first few years querying.

Here are *ten tips* I have for querying your novel, some potentially obvious, some maybe less so, but all important to help you pitch your book effectively and find an agent to represent you...

1. Research, research, research.

There's no way around this one. You have to research every agent you pitch. You need to not only understand what books they represent but also how they want to receive your materials. Does the agent represent your genre? Who are the authors they represent?

And does your agent want you to include a synopsis and the first ten pages of your manuscript, or do they just want the pitch letter and nothing else? There is literally no excuse in screwing up this part. Don't rush the research. It'll help you in the long run.

2. Address the agent by their name.

This one may be the most obvious, but it's simply vital. Do not ever write an e-mail to an agent that starts with DEAR AGENT. You can address the e-mail to either the first name or last name—that part doesn't matter too much—but double check and triple check the spelling is correct.

If you get even one letter wrong, odds will not be in your favor. And finally, double check the gender of the agent. With all the Kellys and Logans out there, never *assume* the agent is male or female.

3. Keep your story pitch to two short paragraphs.

This was the biggest mistake I made my first four years of querying. I always wrote three fairly lengthy paragraphs pitching lots and lots of the story. I spent a year working on the novel, after all, and didn't want to try to sell the book in just 2–4 sentences.

But you know what? Agents are busy people. They get dozens of queries a day. Maybe hundreds. And the more you get to the point, the better chance you'll have to secure their attention. Remember, the point of a query letter is to get the agent to *request pages.*

That's it. That's all. Don't overthink it. You want to be concise, never lengthy. In 2015 I queried a novel with only two sentences about the story, and I got nearly a dozen requests. Which was about ten more requests than the novel I had pitched the year before, which had three giant paragraphs of story in it. When in doubt, *less is more.*

4. Reveal who your main character is.

The first part of your story pitch should tell the agent who your protagonist is. What age? What gender? What occupation? You need to say right away whose story this is.

If the agent gets to the end of your query letter having no idea who the main character is, there's a problem. This should not be a mystery in any way, shape, or form.

5. Reveal the big decision the main character has to make.

It's not enough to say a little about the protagonist and then go on to describe the genre of your work and what other titles it might compare to. Right at the beginning of pitching your story, you need to not only set up who your protagonist is but also what they want.

What is the motivation of this character? What makes them tick? This doesn't necessarily have to be the very first sentence of your story pitch, but it needs to be there somewhere early on, at least by the end of the first paragraph.

6. Reveal the consequences of that decision.

The agent probably won't request pages if there's no conflict presented in your story pitch. You want to hook the agent in by presenting what happens to your character after making that decision, *and* the dilemma and obstacles the character ultimately faces.

You should end your second story paragraph by suggesting a choice your protagonist needs to make that the agent simply must know the answer to. You want to leave the agent on a cliffhanger so that, at the very least, they want to request pages to see what might happen next.

7. Follow the story pitch by a short paragraph detailing what kind of novel you've written.

In the last five books I queried, I kept this paragraph to two sentences. The first sentence says the word count and the genre. Typically, something like "Such and Such is a young adult thriller, complete at 72,000 words and available at your request."

In the second sentence I would compare my book to at least two other titles, something like "My novel would appeal to fans of…" and then name drop a couple of well-received *recent* books you think are similar to your own.

8. End the query with a short note about you, but don't go overboard.

This is not the place to write fifteen sentences about every award you've won and every literary magazine you've been published in. I'd suggest two sentences, three at most.

If you're pursuing an MFA in Creative Writing, mention that. If you've been published in a few magazines, mention two or three of them. But at this point, you really want to keep it short, and let the story pitch speak for itself.

9. Start by querying only a few agents, then query widely if you get requests.

Here's the sad truth of querying agents with your novel: you've got one shot. You can't query an agent your book in February, then in May write a better query for the same novel and try that agent a second time. I mean, you *can*, but it's frowned upon, and you will probably be ignored.

Another important point: it's important to query widely. I've heard of people who queried ten agents, and when they received ten rejections, they gave up. That's ludicrous. You want to reach as many appropriate agents as you can, but at the same time, you don't want to query 100 agents on your first day. What if your query letter has an embarrassing typo? What if two weeks later you want to revise your story pitch?

My method is always this: five queries a week, each week, for a month. By the end of the month, after twenty queries, if I have at least *two requests*, a 10% positive response, then I spend the next two weeks querying *every other agent* on my list. If you know the query is working, then it's in your best interest to query widely, because if an agent offers you representation and you've only queried five people, you can't then query everyone else. You can only reach out to the five you've already queried.

10. Pitch Your Book on Twitter Contests

Lastly, look around on Twitter for Manuscript Wishlist postings—sometimes an agent will post a new Manuscript Wishlist (#MSWL) tweet that closely reflects the book you're getting ready to pitch—and then you want to put #MSWL in the Subject Line of your query letter.

Also look into different Twitter contests that are held occasionally year-round, like #PitMad, #KidPit, #PitDark, #DVPit, and lots more. In 2016 a book I had essentially given up on got about ten agent likes from a single #DVPit tweet. That book isn't the one that eventually got me an agent, but it was exciting to see so much interest in a project two years after I had completely given up on querying it.

Remember, no matter what, to have fun!

Don't take rejection personally. Sometimes no matter how well written your query letter, how commercial your project, how enticing the story, many agents won't respond, and that's okay.

But if you marry an excellent query letter with an amazing novel, you *will* find representation eventually, and you'll have a book in the world one day soon.

My last piece of advice about querying? While you're pitching your novel, do what I always did, something that forever kept me sane…

Write your next book.

79. Why Finding a Literary Agent is Difficult but Worth It

If you want to sell your novels to traditional publishers, it's really difficult to do so on your own. There are ways, of course. You can send your work to small presses oftentimes without an agent. You can send your novel to contests and then be published if you win (one of my novels was once named first runner-up in a novel competition—so close!).

But if you want your book to be pitched to editors at the *major* publishing houses, you have to sign with a literary agent. And the way to do that is to query agents a short pitch of your novel.

Once you learn how to write a fantastic query letter, you're already ahead of the game. The problem with so many writers is that they spend months and months on their novel, then take half an hour to write a terrible query letter that won't get them anywhere.

Remember that the whole point of the query letter is for the literary agent to *request pages*, to get them to actually look at your work. Only then will you get a shot at eventually signing with someone.

The problem is, of course, that it's extremely difficult to find literary representation.

There's a *lot* of competition out there. Agents get hundreds of query letters every week, possibly every day. They can't say yes to everyone. In fact, if everything doesn't come together in the way it should, the likely answer from an agent is going to be no.

It took me *so damn long* to sign with an agent I thought often about giving up. There was a novel that got me twenty full requests from literary agents—*twenty!*—and then they all said no in the ensuing six months.

If anything cuts you down as a writer, it's getting to the point where you *think* you might finally be hitting a milestone in your writing life after years of hard work, only for it not to happen after all.

Unless you're super lucky, the journey to finding a literary agent is in no way an easy one. Just because you write a good novel and write a good query letter doesn't necessarily mean you'll sign with an agent. You might get full requests… but no offers. You might not get any full requests at all (that happened to me with three of my queried novels).

You might get an offer from an agent… but have to say no if the fit doesn't seem right. I've certainly heard of this happening before.

You might find difficulty searching for a literary agent. The key is to let all the rejections slide off your back and keep going, whether that means sending out more query letters of your current novel or writing a new novel and eventually sending query letters out for that one.

Do what you need to do. Because signing with a literary agent is worth it in the end.

It might take you a few books and a few hundred query letters before you sign with a literary agent. The day it comes is super exciting, and then in the weeks to come you will likely be pushed to your limits as a writer from your literary agent.

Once you sign with an agent, success isn't imminent necessarily. And your book likely won't go out on submission right away.

Instead you'll likely need to do a few more revisions with your agent before they begin pitching it. The reason for this is you only get *one chance* to go on submission to editors, and you want to make it count.

To go out too early is like shooting yourself in the foot. You want your book to be the best it can be. And your agent will be a huge help with all that.

Once your agent begins pitching your novel, the excitement returns… at least for a little while. But then there's a lot of waiting involved, again unless you're *super lucky*.

Every part of the process is difficult. Writing the first draft. Revising the book. Querying agents. Revising with the agent. Waiting on responses from editors.

But it's also all necessary and so totally worth it. Whatever part of the process you're in as a novel writer, keep going.

And don't give up!

80. Why You Should Never Query Your Book as a Series

I know, I know, you might be compelled to pitch your novel to literary agents as a series.

Why shouldn't you, after all, since series is truly where the money is when it comes to book publishing.

Unless you're one of the really, really lucky ones who hit it big, stand-alone novels can often struggle in terms of sales. And series, which readers clearly love, are often where authors make the big bucks.

Think back on the biggest publishing phenomena of the past twenty years. *Harry Potter. Twilight. The Hunger Games. Jack Reacher. Alex Cross. Outlander.*

All series. All written by authors who have made millions and millions of dollars.

People working in the publishing industry are always looking for the next big series, and so it should be in the back of your mind to attempt a series of books sooner or later. I definitely have. I've written and self-published two trilogies on Amazon. And I've written at least three books since that I definitely set up for sequels at the end.

If you're written the first installment of a series, you might be compelled in your query letters to say it's the start of a trilogy, or the start of a five-book series, of whatever you think it may be.

Ultimately though, you'll have more success if you pitch your novel as a stand-alone.

And going a step further, I would suggest you write the novel in a way that makes it so that it *could* continue into a second book but that it could also *end* in book one. Find some middle ground there if at all possible.

Because here's the deal: pitching a series right off the bat can scare potential agents and/or editors away, and so what you should do instead is write the best book you can and let it stand on its own merits.

Agents might not take a chance on you if they feel that you're only interested in writing a series and not a stand-alone. Furthermore, that agent might take you on, but then an editor might only be interested in purchasing the first installment from you and *not* any sequels. You might spend all this time setting things up for part two when your editors wants you to wrap things up at the end of part one!

You'll be better off in the long run by capturing the magic of your story as best you can in the first installment, instead of putting yourself in a position where a series contract is required.

At the same time, you want to be ambitious in your novel writing career, too.

You want to sometimes think about writing a series. Be ambitious and think big! But you also need to be smart about how you go about this process. You might imagine a seven-book series, but it's probably best you keep that to yourself, at least for now.

If you put in your query letter that your novel is the first in a seven-book series, you will struggle finding an agent, I guarantee you. You might get lucky with one person who believes in you, especially if the writing is strong, but you don't want to shoot yourself in the foot like this ever.

Now you could write a sentence near the bottom of your query letter like this: *[Title] would appeal to readers of [such and such] and could be the first of a series.* I don't think it hurts to vaguely point to the book having series potential.

The problem is when you write a sentence like, *[Title] is the first of a seven-book series, all six sequels of which I've heavily outlined, and I can send you those outlines if you'd like as well.*

Don't this! You might think you're standing out from the crowd in a good way, but usually sentences like these won't get you anywhere and might even scare some agents off.

When in doubt, let the agent fall in love with your book so much that when they ask you later on if it could be the first of a series, you can give them an unequivocal yes!

One other thing: do not, under any circumstances, write the sequels before you sell the first book!

If you're self-publishing, go all out. Write twenty books of your series. Series are huge in the self-publishing world.

But if you're querying your novel to literary agents, don't waste your time in the following few weeks or months writing parts two and three.

You might think you're saving time by writing book two now because you just *know* your first book's going to sell later in a two-book deal where a sequel is going to be requested… but the editor or even the agent might not like the direction your second installment goes in, and all that work might have been for nothing.

If you're aiming for traditional publishing and want your latest project to be a series, the best thing you can do is write an awesome first book that could be a stand-alone but also has enough of an open ending that it could continue as well.

Remember to stay ambitious, think big, and be *smart* when it comes to the world of book publishing. You'll be glad you did!

81. Be Wary of Literary Agents Who Demand a Fee from You

One more thing to be said about literary agents? Don't work with any who demand a fee up front.

Yes, literary agents work really, really hard. And yes, they deserve to get paid.

But the way it works is this. You query your novel to multiple literary agents, which costs you, the writer, no money. You might receive partial or full requests from literary agents who want to see more of your work. You promptly send the requested pages to the agent, and then they read your work *for no money*.

If you're lucky, one or more of those agents will offer you representation, and hopefully you'll be able to accept one of those offers. Then you'll begin the revising process of your novel with that agent, again, *for no money*.

Throughout this process you shouldn't be paying your agent anything. You should never be pressured into paying then a dime.

The only time the agent gets paid is if your novel sells, and then that agent gets a percentage.

I believe the industry standard is 15% for the sale to the publisher, and then 20% for any foreign sales / film options / and the rest. The agent makes money when *you* make money, that's how it works. That's what you should always keep at the back of your mind as you search for representation.

One other thing you should keep at the back of your mind? There will be people out there who want to take advantage of you. Who will feed off your desperation to get an agent, to get published, that after awhile you might feel it's okay to pay an agent to read your work or that it's okay to pay an agent before your book is pitched to editors.

This is not okay. This is not a person you should be working with. Any agent who does something like this will probably be out of the job eventually as soon as the complaints start rolling in, but you never know. Anyone can become a literary agent, after all.

Your job is to seek out the ones that will help guide your career and get your books published, and avoid the ones that are scam artists.

The only agents worth considering are the ones that don't demand any fees up front, remember that.

I don't care if you've queried five novels and finally found someone who's interested in your work. I don't care if you've been at this for years, and one particular agent is interested in your novel… for a fee. Don't do it! Do *not* work with this person!

At the end of the day, there's one last thing to keep in the back of your mind: it's better to not have an agent at all than to have a bad agent. It's better to have no agent than to have an agent who scams you for money and gives you nothing in return!

Searching for a literary agent is an exciting time, but you need to remember to keep your business hat on always. Make good choices. Do your research.

There are lots of literary agents out there. Work with the good ones.

82. 5 Things You Should Know if You Want to Self Publish Your Novel

Self publishing is something every novel writer should look into sooner or later.

Because you know what? Self publishing has changed considerably in the past ten years, even the past five years. It's not looked at in the kind of negative light it used to be.

Sure, there is a whole lot of crap getting self published out there in 2020, but there's also a lot of quality novels finding homes with readers everywhere.

Self publishing doesn't have to be embarrassing. It doesn't have to mean a death sentence. I've been trying to be traditionally published for a long time because I hope to see my book on a Barnes & Noble shelf and I want to work with amazing literary agents and editors that will help take my writing to the highest level possible.

But I've also thought about self publishing more than ever as of late. I currently have ten novels in the drawer — that's right, *ten novels* that have never seen the light of day — and part of me is wondering if it's finally time to get to work on putting at least some of these manuscripts into the world.

You can self publish anything you want, but the trick to be successful is to do it the right way, not the wrong way. Trust me, I've done it the wrong way many times before, and I don't want to self publish one of my novels again until I have a solid plan and some talented people to help me make the writing soar.

Here are the *five things* you should know if you want to self publish your novel…

1. You want the entire package to be as professional as possible.

This is number one. You're not going to want to slack on anything. Self publishing your novel is not the time to do a quick read-through, throw together a decent cover, and call it a day.

You have to treat the self publishing of your novel, even if it's just one novel, as a business. You want to be professional. You want to look like you know what you're doing.

Keep in mind there are so many novels self published these days. How are you going to stand out? What's going to make a reader care about your book? If it's not thoroughly professional in every way, you're never going to make much of an impression on anyone.

2. If you're not adept at graphic design, hire someone to design your cover.

One of the first things your potential readers are going to see is your novel's cover. Again, this is not the time to slap something together that's mediocre or that doesn't represent your novel as well as it could.

Unless you're super skilled at graphic design, you shouldn't be making your cover in the first place. You should *hire* someone to make a cover for you. I'm lucky enough to have a longtime friend who's super skilled at graphic design, but there are lots of places you can pay people to do the exact cover you want. There are even places where you can pay money to have various people *compete* to be your graphic designer.

I know you want to save money. I know you want to find some free public domain image and put some fancy text on it. I see these kinds of covers all the time, but they won't do you any favors. Your cover is going to tell your reader how serious you are about self publishing. Make sure the cover is pure gold!

3. If you have some money in your budget, hire an editor or at least a copyeditor.

I wouldn't suggest it's as important to hire an editor for your novel than it is to hire a graphic designer to make your cover, but if you have some money in the budget, it wouldn't hurt for you to hire an editor to help make your manuscript better in every aspect.

Even just hiring a copyeditor to go through the book and find all the typos and misspellings will give your work the professional polish it needs. Do you ever notice typos and misspellings in traditionally published books? Almost never, right? And when you do, it always sticks out because seeing one is so rare.

An occasional typo or misspelling won't bring your self published novel down, but several will absolutely hurt you in the eyes of the reader. You want them to get lost in your story. You don't want the magic evaporating for them every few pages because of constant errors in your manuscript. Editors will help with this, and, again, if you have the money, they're well worth it in the end.

4. Series sell much better than stand-alone novels, and publishing books in the same genre will help grow your success, too.

A big reason I've hesitated self publishing lots of the novels I've written in the past few years is that they're all stand-alone books. They don't have sequels, don't have follow-ups. And those can be hard sells when it comes to the self publishing world.

Readers love series. They love to go on a journey with characters in not just one book but in several. Trilogies are good. Series of five books or more are even better! If you want to be a success at self publishing, it's going to be in your best interest to write series instead of stand-alone novels, although it's certainly possible to write a stand-alone book that sells a lot of copies.

Keep in mind that your genre is important, too. A mystery or a thriller or a romance book will probably sell better than a super introspective literary novel. Readers have so many options these days, and you want to grab them with something. You want there to be some kind of hook. They don't have time for things they might not understand.

And that goes for the genre you keep self publishing in, too. I made the mistake in my early self publishing days of putting out books in different genres, which absolutely confused my readers. Don't self publish a horror novel, then put out a romance and a western a few months later. If you're going to publish stand-alone novels, at least stay consistent in the *genre* they're categorized in.

———

5. You're going to have to promote, promote, promote.

Here's the last big one. Something you absolutely can't ignore. It's something you need to understand when it comes to traditional publishing, too, but you for sure can't ignore it when it comes to self publishing.

There's always this feeling once you self publish something that because *you* worked on it so hard for so long, the readers are going to show up no matter what. You've revised it a bunch of times, had a copyeditor comb through it, hired a graphic designer to make you an amazing cover. The book is in a popular genre, and it's the first of a trilogy. Naturally you're going to assume hundreds of readers will snap it up instantly.

I'm sad to say that's rarely the case. Even if all the right elements come together, it's very well possible you'll self publish the book and have almost no sales at all. A week will go by, a month will go by. You've told your friends and family… and you've sold less than ten copies. What happened? What went wrong?

Well, what probably went wrong is that you didn't do any effective promotion for the book. You did no marketing of any kind. You didn't spend any money for this part of the process, which is simply essential. Sure, if your novel is really good, you'll probably sell some copies of it eventually even if you don't do any promotion. Some people will find it if you wait long enough, but the problem is most of them won't.

You're going to want to pay for some advertising, and you'll want to promote it on Facebook and Twitter and

Instagram and Amazon and anywhere you can think of. You'll want to try new things *constantly* and see what works well and what doesn't. You can't just sit back and hope readers come. You have to make sure they find your book sooner rather than later!

Whatever novel you're planning to self publish, I wish you only the best with it!

Traditional publishing isn't for everyone, after all. And sometimes you try for traditional publishing for a long while and have no success, but you know in your heart you have an amazing story the world deserves to read.

Just because you never found a literary agent to sign with doesn't mean that novel you adore is over and done with. There's still absolutely a way to get it out there, and better yet, you'll have complete control over it, too!

Self publish for the right reasons and do everything you can to make your work professional. Spend money for the perfect cover, hire an editor or copyeditor if you can, and promote, promote, promote.

And think about writing a series too, not just stand-alone books. Even if you write the best stand-alone novel ever, you won't get very far if you only end up self publishing one book. You should want to self publish lots and lots of books!

And if they're in the same genre, especially in the same series, your chances of success will only increase in the weeks and months to come.

83. 5 Reasons Why You Should Attend an MFA in Creative Writing

Receiving an MFA in Creative Writing in 2018 was one of my greatest accomplishments by far.

It was the conclusion of an eight-year pursuit, first of all. In 2010 I made the decision I wanted to focus on fiction writing the next few years, and I wanted to spend some time in an MFA program to improve in my abilities.

So I applied that fall… and wasn't accepted anywhere. I tried again in 2012 and was accepted to exactly one program… but they didn't have any funding. Finally the stars aligned in 2014 when my local university started its own MFA in Creative Writing, and I was ecstatic to be accepted to its first MFA class of fiction writers.

I had an incredible experience in the MFA in Creative Writing program at the University of Nevada, Reno, between 2015 and 2018. I learned a lot. I worked really hard. I had some great adventures. I met so many amazing people.

I wouldn't trade that experience for anything, and two years out of the program, I certainly miss a few things. So let's talk about the *good* of an MFA, shall we?

Here are five reasons why you *should* pursue an MFA in Creative Writing…

1. Time

This in many ways is the number one reason to do it. When you have a full-time job and you have lots of responsibilities and you have very little time for yourself, it can be hard to ever find quality time to devote to your writing. Sure, you might be able to grab a half-hour here and a half-hour there, but how are you ever going to get better at your craft if you're always cramming in writing sessions whenever they're made available to you?

The great thing about an MFA in Creative Writing is that it allows you two or three years to focus *exclusively* on your writing. It gives you some much needed quiet time to work on the kind of writing that speaks to you, that you feel passion for… and that you finally have the *time* for.

If time is what you're lacking right now, and you're serious about becoming a writer, an MFA in Creative Writing might be exactly what you're looking for.

2. Community

Another excellent part of joining an MFA in Creative Writing is that you become part of a large community of writers. When you're off writing on your own and most everyone in your life doesn't understand what you do, maybe even mocks what you do, it can be really hard to believe in yourself and get any better.

When you sit in rooms with other writers who are pursuing the same dreams you are, you feel better about yourself. You gain more confidence. And it's a gift, really, to find a tribe of like-minded people who love to write and talk about writing. It can be thrilling to develop life-long friends you can root for every step of the way, even after the MFA program has concluded.

I had so many great times with the community I was lucky enough to join in my MFA program in 2015. So many times we helped each other with our writing, so many late nights we spent laughing, so many fun trips to conferences we took together I'll never forget. The MFA in Creative Writing can be an amazing thing because you go from isolation as a writer to being part of a community, and there's truly nothing like it.

3. Connections

Along with community, an MFA in Creative Writing allows you to make helpful connections, both with the professors in your department and with writers that are brought in from the outside. My MFA experience allowed me to get valuable insight into the writing process from at least a dozen knowledgeable and inspiring professors at my school, including a rock star thesis adviser, and they've been helpful after the MFA to get references and letters of recommendations from, too.

Besides the professors themselves, MFA programs often bring in outside writers at least a couple of times a semester for readings, lectures, and personal visits. In my program each year we had an established fiction writer not only give a reading and lecture but also workshop our writing. They would each be at the university for three days or longer, and so those are connections I'll always value.

Joining an MFA in Creative Writing program doesn't necessarily guarantee you connections with literary agents and editors and people like that, but my program had a Publishing & Editing class that had a revolving door of guests from the publishing industry, both in person and via Skype. This seminar taught me so much about the industry and even gave me a few long-lasting connections, too!

4. Credibility

If you're serious about being a writer and want to have your work published in literary magazines, maybe even sign with a literary agent and have a novel published in the future, an MFA in Creative Writing absolutely gives you credibility on all these fronts. While the MFA doesn't *guarantee* any of this, what it does is show people that you're a serious writer and that you've spent a few years dedicating time and energy to the craft.

In effect the MFA gives you some credibility. It's really hard to get accepted to an MFA program, first of all. Many schools receive hundreds of applications and only accept ten or fewer writers a year. It's tough to get in, and then to maintain the loaded course work and complete that colossal thesis project before the degree is finally yours. An MFA isn't easy, and receiving that degree shows the world you've worked tirelessly for years.

And once you apply for job positions later, and when you query literary agents, and when you submit your shorter work to literary magazines, having in your bio that you graduated with an MFA in Creative Writing will certainly help you reach your dreams than if you had no qualifications at all. Sure, the *writing* is what matters most, but having the MFA doesn't hurt you one bit.

5. Improvement

Finally, besides time, there might be no better reason to pursue an MFA in Creative Writing than to improve in your craft. You can only get so far as a writer when your work is merely competent or good. You want to be great. You want the time and community and connections to help make you great, and that's what an MFA in Creative Writing program does.

When I entered my program in 2015, I felt like my writing was solid but could definitely be improved. And through working closely with other students, professors, and visiting writers, and taking more than ten workshops and writing seminars, my writing reached a level by 2018 I never thought was possible. My MFA thesis novel, for example, was something I never thought I had the talent or ability to pull off, but through lots of hard work and help from others, that novel is now everything I hoped it would be.

You'll learn in an MFA program about literary writing versus genre writing, you'll study character and setting and theme more closely, you'll read and discuss lots of amazing books you might never have found on your own, you'll discover the crucial importance of revision. If you want to improve as a writer? An MFA in Creative Writing is something worth looking into, it's as simple as that.

Keep in mind that an MFA in Creative Writing isn't right for everyone.

It's definitely not the be all and end all. You don't have to pursue an MFA if you want to be a writer. Again, many successful writers don't have an MFA. Some don't even have English degrees of any kind!

An MFA in Creative Writing doesn't guarantee anything, and every MFA program is different. I was lucky enough to attend a program that welcomed genre writing, so I felt at home writing horror short stories and young adult novels. Many MFA programs wouldn't have even allowed me to write these things, so if genre writing is your thing, you'll have to think twice about what you want to do.

Whatever you plan on doing, hopefully this list gives you some insight into the most positive aspects of an MFA in Creative Writing from someone who's actually gone through one. Whether or not you pursue an MFA, I wish you the best of luck in your writing!

84. 5 Reasons Why an MFA in Creative Writing Might Not Be for You

An MFA in Creative Writing is certainly worth your time if you go into it for the right reasons.

If you want a few years to dedicate to your craft, an MFA in Creative Writing is a solid option. It's also helpful for building a community and finding connections and giving you some credibility. And it's of course a great way to help improve your writing.

But is an MFA in Creative Writing a crucial pursuit if you want to be a successful fiction writer? Absolutely not. So many people have built amazing careers and become huge successes in their writing lives without an MFA. You don't have to do it if you don't want to, so now let's take a look at the negative side.

Here are a few *bad* reasons to pursue an MFA in Creative Writing...

1. You think it guarantees you a tenure-track professor position at the college level.

One myth I firmly believed when I applied for and eventually pursued an MFA in Creative Writing was that the degree would give me a huge boost to obtaining a tenure-track teaching job at the college level. I didn't necessarily think it guaranteed me anything, but I assumed having the MFA in Creative Writing on my CV would mean huge things in the coming years when I applied for teaching positions.

Well, two years since I received my MFA, I've applied for more than fifty teaching positions all around the country, and I've had exactly one interview. I've had help with my cover letter and CV from many writer friends and professors since 2018, and I at least thought I could be competitive at obtaining interviews, but the truth is the response has mostly been silence. And that response can be defeating when you work your ass off for three years to be met only with shrugs from the important decision makers you apply to.

Many people have told me that what I'm lacking is a traditionally published novel, and I think to a large part that's true. It's not for a lack of trying. I signed with a literary agent in 2017 and we tried to sell something for more than a year. I received second place in a novel competition that *almost* got one of my novels traditionally published. I've come close so often, but sadly in 2020 I'm still trying, and it's going to be hard for me to find a tenure-track teaching job at this time.

Now, this has just been my experience, and it might well be different for you. A friend of mine from my MFA program did secure a tenure-track teaching job at a community college, without a published novel in the world, so that certainly gives me hope for the future. And if you want to get a full-time teaching position at the college level, you'll need at least an MA degree, remember that. But I wouldn't pursue an MFA in Creative Writing if an eventual teaching job was your *sole reason* for doing so.

2. You believe it guarantees your work will be accepted to more publications.

Like I discussed before, obtaining an MFA in Creative Writing degree helps your credibility to a certain extent. It shows people whom you're applying to or submitting work to that you take writing seriously and that your work will likely outshine the work of many others. But does getting an MFA guarantee you'll finally get your writing published? Unfortunately the answer is no. Not a single editor of a literary magazine will take on that story you submitted just because they see in your bio that you have an MFA. It's all about the writing.

Now, what an MFA program *can* help with is improving your writing through the workshop process. When you're in an MFA program you'll take many workshops where you bring a draft of a short story and have the other students in the class, along with the professor, read your work and give you lots of feedback. Not all of that feedback will be helpful, but much of it will be, and you'll be able to get valuable insight into the work that helps you shape it into something better.

That's the side of an MFA program that might help you get more of your work published, but, again, there's no guarantee of anything. An editor might pleasingly nod at the detail in your bio that you have an MFA, but then that person is going to read your writing and make the decision solely based on the quality or lack thereof. Don't think you can slack in any way, whether or not you have an MFA.

3. You think it guarantees you'll be able to sign with a literary agent.

Many aspiring writers pursue an MFA in Creative Writing because they have dreams of signing with a literary agent and getting their first novel published. Yes, this has certainly happened before in the long history of MFA in Creative Writing programs. Some have been lucky to get an agent by the time they graduate and then possibly get their novel published soon after. Literary agents are always looking for the next fresh voice, and many of those voices will come out of MFA programs.

But just like when it comes to editors of literary magazines, a literary agent won't sign you if the writing isn't stellar, if it doesn't move them, if they don't know how they can sell the work. The MFA degree will only get you so far with literary agents, and you must be willing to put in the time and hard work to get your writing to the best possible place it can be.

If what you really want as a writer is a novel writing career where you eventually sign with a literary agent and get your work published? You don't necessarily need an MFA for that. Unless you take a publishing seminar that's offered, most of the work you do in an MFA program is improving your writing, not finding connections to the publishing industry or teaching you how to query a novel. You can read books for that, attend conferences for that.

There are lots of ways into a successful writing career outside of an MFA program.

4. You believe the debt you'll accumulate doesn't matter.

I was lucky to join an MFA program that left me with no debt. Where all but one semester I paid less than $500 in tuition. In fact, one year I won a writing prize that gave me money toward my tuition, and the following year of the program I owed *nothing* in tuition. I received teaching assistantships that paid me enough to survive and that gave me health insurance. And when I graduated in 2018, again, I left not owing any money to the university.

I would strongly advise against pursuing an MFA in Creative Writing in a program that offered no TA-ships or financial help. The one MFA program I was accepted to in 2012 was a three-year program at $20,000 a year, and in my second and final phone call with the head of the program I was informed it was *possible* to get a TA-ship the second and third years but that it was in no way certain.

That was too much of a gamble to take. $60,000 for an MFA in Creative Writing? I wasn't about to spend that kind of money toward a degree that offered no guarantees. And as much as I loved the college and the program, I had to pass. Well, I'm glad I did because two years later I got into an awesome program that cost me almost nothing and gave me so much in return!

So unless you have the financial means to do whatever the hell you want, I would only pursue MFA programs that leave you with little or no debt. You want your writing to be the focus, after all, and you don't want to have the stress of trying to pay for so much out of pocket semester after semester.

5. You think the community and connections you make will be forever.

One thing that's both magical and heartbreaking about an MFA program is that eventually it has to end. And when it does, everything changes. Sure, you get to take with you what you got out of it, especially when it comes to the improvement of your own writing, but when it comes to the people you worked with and engaged with on a weekly basis, that community you helped build is unfortunately no more.

Yes, you will make life-long connections and friendships in an MFA program. I certainly made a few of them. But my best friends from the program all moved away after we graduated, and so there's no longer that face-to-face connection that made every semester in the program such a pleasure.

The same goes with all the professors you work with. Sure, you'll follow many of them on Facebook, you'll write each other e-mails at times, but for the most part they're busy with the new MFA students and you're sort of on your own path now. They'll always be there for you if you need them, but you're no longer a priority.

So if you're pursuing an MFA program strictly for the community and connections, keep in mind they don't last forever. If you're super lucky, maybe you'll keep a smaller version of that community going long after you graduate, but for the most part, people go their separate ways.

So please—pursue an MFA in Creative Writing for the right reasons.

If this is something you want to do, then go for it, but don't do it solely because you want a tenure-track teaching job, or because you want to get published more often, or because you want to sign with a literary agent. An MFA program is also not worth going into debt for, and keep in mind that the community and connections you make in the program aren't necessarily forever.

Instead, do it for the time that allows you to be creative and find your writing voice. Do it for the community you'll be a part of and the connections you'll make during the program. Do it to give you some more credibility and to help improve in your craft.

And one last thing to keep in mind, too—there are *so many* MFA in Creative Writing programs out there. If it's something you're serious about, do your research and only pursue the ones that work well for you. And if you don't want to pursue an MFA? That's fine, too. You can still be a successful writer without an MFA, never forget that.

Whatever you end up doing, whether you pursue an MFA in Creative Writing or not, I wish you only the best. Keep writing, keep improving. And never give up!

85. Remember that Writing Classes Aren't Magic Bullets to Success

I'm a little more positive about writing classes and seminars than other people are.

I should be, obviously, since I spent many years in graduate school, took dozens of writing classes, and have been to many writing conferences throughout the years. There is absolutely something to be said about the benefits to these things.

For me, I always walk away from a good writing class or seminar super inspired to write to my heart's content. If I'm ever in a funk, all I need is an hour or two listening to people talk about writing or engage in a conversation about a great book or short story with some colleagues in an intimate environment.

Writing is a lonely job. Sometimes it's nice to sit with a group of people and talk about writing. Share each other's work. Give feedback. Talk about character development, conflict, backstory, pacing, etc. Finding other people who have your interests is always a benefit to your creative life.

It's nice to know when you're in year three, year four, year five, of writing every day that there are other crazies just like you in the world!

However, writing classes and seminars are definitely not magic bullets, so you need to be careful.

If you're struggling as a writer, one really awesome writing seminar isn't going to make you successful. A class you attend in the fall on Mondays and Wednesdays isn't necessarily going to make you sell your book either. There's no guarantee with anything in writing. and you can't look at classes and seminars as ways to ensure everything works out.

I've been to writing seminars where I see people all around me jotting down *every single word* the speaker says, and I'm always left wondering if they ever work this hard at home when they're by themselves and have a blank page on the laptop in front of them.

The big truth about writing classes and seminars is this: they don't in any way replace good old-fashioned practice, practice, practice. You can talk about writing until the end of time but doing so is never going to make you improve as a writer.

You get better by actually *writing*. If the class you're in requires you to produce two or three short stories (or novel excerpts), that's always helpful because you're essentially forced to produce.

But when it comes to conferences and seminars, typically you pay a lot of money to sit in a room for a day or two and listen to people talk about writing. Again, one of these here and there can be inspiring for writers, almost necessary. But they also don't replace the need for you to write.

So make sure your writing takes center stage, while classes and seminars remain in the background.

Sure, classes and seminars can actually take time away from your writing, which, in the end, is more useful in your career, and—cough—*free*.

Don't let classes and seminars replace your writing. Instead let them be *supplements* to your vast creative life. Take a creative writing class to make some new friends and get fresh pairs of eyeballs on your current work. Go to a conference once a year if it gives you a jolt of inspiration. There's no harm in that at all.

But be careful you don't ever immerse yourself in these settings to the point where talking about writing takes over, and the *actual writing* becomes lost in the shuffle.

The best thing you can do every day? Sit your ass down and write.

And eventually you'll get to the place you want to be!

86. Why You Need to be Cautious about Workshop Critiques

It's sad but true: I would argue that at times workshop critiques can be harmful to writers rather than helpful.

I've been a part of a lot of creative writing workshops. I took my first one in the spring of 2012 and my last one in the spring of 2017. In five years of graduate school, I took part in ten semester-long workshops. *Ten*!

Some of these experiences were great. Others… weren't so great.

The best workshop settings I took part in had less than ten students. My Spring 2016 semester I took a night workshop with just six other fiction writers, and all six of them were so smart and generous with their time. The advice they gave me for the three stories I submitted that semester were spot-on and super helpful.

However, I also took a workshop in the fall of 2012 that didn't go so well.

The class was comprised of twenty-two students, all of them in different stages of writing, and I would say maybe five of the twenty-one responses I received on my stories were helpful. Many of them though were super vague to the point where I wondered if some of the students even read my story.

I was never mad about this, exactly. I mean, it makes sense. Each of us that semester had to turn in two short stories, so that meant we had to read and respond to *forty-two* stories during the course of four months. It was a lot.

When you have only six other students in the class, there's actual time to learn the strengths and weaknesses of each writer and what they can do to improve.

Twenty-two students is more of a crowd than a class, particularly when it comes to the workshop setting. Any workshop larger than fifteen students becomes too chaotic, and after a certain point you have to be a little vague here and there with your comments just to survive the semester.

The worst thing you can do for your next draft is try to incorporate the advice of every single critique!

Whether your workshop is comprised of seven students or twenty-two students, you can't possibly integrate all that feedback. It'll drive you mad to do so, and it will make your story or novel so much worse.

Here's what you should do instead. First, take an afternoon and read through *all* the comments, checking or underlining or highlighting any feedback you agree with. Second, once you've read through all the responses, now look over what you marked up and make a new Word document and type up all the feedback you want to integrate into the next draft.

Always start with the most valuable feedback of all (usually notes that many of the workshop students included in their critiques) and then work your way down.

As long as you don't try to integrate everything, you're on the path to a better draft. Use the feedback that makes sense, that you agree with, and toss the feedback that's too vague or makes no sense or that you strongly disagree with.

Creative writing workshops can be helpful, but you should also be cautious when it comes to the critiques.

Just be *smart* at the end of the day and do what you need to do to make your latest work of fiction its absolute best!

87. How to Get the Most Out of a Writing Conference

When I started writing fiction in 2010, I thought there was one thing I needed to do to get published.

All I was going to have to do was write a great book and send out a tantalizing query letter to literary agents. I didn't need to be social to be a writer, after all.

I didn't have to go to parties or any literary events. And I *certainly* didn't have to go to conferences.

When I moved back to Reno in early 2011, my grandfather Ralph told me about a one-day writer's conference being held at the local community college on a Saturday and suggested I go. "Maybe you'll meet some other writers," he told me. "Maybe you'll learn something."

I had such an ego in 2011, three novels completed, and an offer of representation soon to come, I assumed, that I skipped the conference, not thinking I needed it. I spent the rest of 2011 holed up in my room writing—I wrote the first drafts for five different novels that year, still a record. And while I was producing a ton, I wasn't learning an important part of the writing process that isn't talked about much—being part of a larger community.

Whether someone is focused on creative writing or scholarly writing—or both, like many graduate students—making new contacts and connections play a major role in a successful writing career.

After I took my first writing workshop in the spring of 2012, I learned that maybe I *did* need to branch out of my bedroom and seek help to better my writing. I went to the community college writing conference for the first time in 2012 and have attended many years since.

In 2012 and 2013 I also started attending writing conferences outside of Reno.

In the summer of 2012, I attended a writer's conference in Los Angeles called RWA. This was a romance writer's conference that had about five other men in its pool of at least two thousand attendees.

I definitely felt like a fish out of water at that one, but some of the talks—including one about LGBTQ content in young adult fiction—certainly hooked me, and the conference also gave me the opportunity to spend a whole afternoon pitching agents my latest novel.

It was absolutely terrifying to spend ten minutes telling my story to an agent who could potentially read it and sign me as a client, and while I didn't get an agent in the end, I certainly welcomed the experience.

In 2013, I went to a different writer's conference in Los Angeles—SCBWI, which I've attended twice and have absolutely loved since my first morning soaking in the inspiration from working writers of children's fiction.

I've spent some surreal hours at SCBWI in LA—picking the brain of Stephen Chbosky, the author of *The Perks of Being a Wallflower*, and talking LGBT content in children's fiction with Tim Federle, the author of one of my favorite middle-grade novels, *Better Nate Than Ever*.

Since my passion is YA, I count myself lucky to have found a community in SCBWI that wants each one of its members to succeed.

Writing conferences inspire me in so many ways. They've helped me better my writing. They've allowed me to tell other writers I admire how much I respect their work. And they're absolutely worth investing time in for you, too.

But keep in mind there's a smart way of going about a writing conference and a way that won't get you very far.

How, ultimately, do you get the *most* out of a writing conference?

Here are five strategies that have worked for me over the years, and I think they might work for you, too.

1. Plan Ahead

I put this one first because it's a big one. Sure, you can't plan for *everything*. Sometimes you'll plan on two panels you want to see back-to-back… and then right before that first panel, you'll get a phone call from a friend you haven't seen in two years and all those plans you made the night before are now thrown out the window.

But that's okay. Sometimes plans change. What helps me a lot in the days leading up to a conference is taking some downtime to go through the conference catalogue and circling everything I want to go to while I'm there. I circle every panel that looks interesting, any reading I feel I can't miss.

Going a step further, I also look up coffeehouses and restaurants around the conference, places I'll be able to step away for an hour or more to hydrate and get my energy back up.

The more you know about your conference before you go will make your trip all the better in the long run. There won't be hours of wandering through the conference halls trying to figure out what to do. There won't be panic at 2pm trying to find a place to have lunch.

You can always change your plans later. But have some kind of set plan so you at least have an idea of what you want to do with your days at the conference.

2. Take Lots of Breaks

This one is huge, I tell you. Maybe even more important than number one. If you don't take at least the occasional break throughout the day, *you will burn out*, and you will regret the past seven hours when you just couldn't stop.

Trust me, I get it. You've paid a lot for the conference. You paid to fly or drive to the conference, and to stay somewhere. Most conferences I've been to are only two or three days.

You don't have a lot of time. And there's so much great stuff to see.

Yes, I know. You want to take advantage of *every single minute*.

The first major writers conference I attended was the SCBWI Conference in Los Angeles in 2013. The first day I went from 8am to about 8pm without taking a single break. I had a bar for breakfast and a bar for lunch. I ran out of water in the late afternoon. But there was so much cool stuff I just couldn't stop.

You know what happened next? I went home, ate a super late dinner, then crashed and didn't return to the conference until the following afternoon. The previous day exhausted me to the point where I couldn't possibly do it all over again, and I don't even think I stayed very long at the conference the second day. That first day had completely done me in.

What you should do at your conference is *pace yourself*. Don't try to see every single panel between 9am and 7pm. Don't try to see all twelve of your friends that are attending the conference in one day.

Have breakfast before you arrive to the conference. Then take an hour break, at least, to have lunch.

And instead of that late afternoon panel, maybe get some coffee or tea with a friend. Go find a sofa and take a nap. Hell, feel free to go back to your hotel room or Airbnb in the middle of the day to recharge!

You need to take breaks to get the most out of a conference. Don't ever think that you don't.

3. Make Some New Connections

This is the most difficult strategy to implement at a conference, at least for me.

You take a seat in the audience for a panel, and there are five or ten more minutes to go before it begins. You look around at a sea of strangers. Faces you've never seen before. You could maybe start up a conversation with someone sitting next to you, but instead you take out your journal and pretend to write something, or you take out your phone and scroll through Facebook and Twitter.

I get this. I'm a writer. I like to be alone, and I'm not great at meeting new people.

I'm afraid I'll say the wrong thing. I don't want to be rejected. It's so much easier to stay quiet.

But here's the thing about writing conferences: most everyone attending the thing is *just like you*. Everyone else is shy, too. And better yet, everybody's a writer, so there's automatically something to talk about!

At my first conference I didn't say a word to anybody, and I left that weekend without a single new connection. The following year, I literally *forced myself* to start talking to people. It was really, really hard, but I did it.

And you know what happened? I walked away from that second conference with at least ten new connections, plus two people who are still my friends to this day!

You don't have to go out of your way to do this. You don't need to walk up to random people in the hallway and start chatting.

Start with baby steps. Turn to the person next to you in the audience for a panel and say hi. Next? If that person next to you is a writer—and of course, most people attending a writing conference *are*—they will probably say a few words about their work. And then you can go from there.

Sometimes the conversation is limited. I've begun conversations with a few people at conferences that led nowhere. But sometimes they *do* lead somewhere, and it's in your best interest to at least try to make some connections.

4. Reconnect with Friends

I'll be the first to admit I spent more time with friends at the 2019 AWP Writers Conference, which took place in Portland, Oregon, than the conference itself. On Friday, the second major day of the conference, I went to exactly one panel, and spent the rest of the day touching base with one old friend of mine after another.

I even reconnected with a friend from elementary school I hadn't seen in twenty-three years!

You don't have to spend all day in panels. Sometimes, certainly in the case of AWP, there's so much great stuff it's hard enough just to pick among all the amazing panels being offered, and it almost seems wrong in a way to skip any of them.

But in my experience, going from one panel to the next *wears me out*. I don't retain as much information as I could if, again, I took a break here and there.

Instead of going to six panels back to back, I usually pick *three* to check out. One in the morning. One around noon. One in the afternoon. This is how I go about my writing conferences now, and I feel I have more success that way.

The more years you write, and the more years you make writer friends, you will have a select group of people to spend time with at big conferences like AWP.

If there's someone attending that you know, make the effort to reach out to them! Sometimes it's nice after a long day of panels to reconnect with a familiar face.

Occasionally you'll attend a conference where you don't know anybody attending. That's happened to me before. If that's the case, see #3. Even if every other attendee is a stranger, that doesn't mean they all have to be strangers for long.

5. Get Enough Sleep

At AWP I slept eight hours both nights at my Airbnb. It was glorious.

And pretty easy, especially when you spend ten hours or more on your feet and talking to friends and being inspired by great writers in panels throughout the day. Both nights I crashed at about 11pm and then woke up around 7am. This made the conference all the more successful.

If you stay out that first night until 3am partying and drinking with friends, that's fine and all, but I guarantee you that next day is *not* going to be successful.

You probably won't get to the conference until noon or later, and you won't be totally on your game when it comes to the panels and meeting new people.

Again, conferences are usually pretty short. You only have two or three days. Party it up after the conference is over. Party it up *next* weekend.

Use your time at a writers conference wisely. And get enough sleep. You don't want to walk around the place like a zombie on days two and three.

You want to be totally alert for everything great and special and *spectacular* that's still to come your way!

88. Why Being Taken Seriously as a Writer is So Important

Writing is hard enough. Being looked at with condescension from others makes it even harder.

Being a writer is a hard life, there's no doubt about it. There's no financial stability. There's lots of rejection, *so much* rejection. You stare at blank pages every day in the hopes that you'll be able to fill it up with something great. There are many, many days when the writing doesn't go well and you feel like a total failure.

And what makes all this even harder? When you have people in your life, particularly friends and family, who look at what you do and what you love with pitying condescension. Who look at you with sorrow as soon as you're asked what you do and you say that you're a writer.

I *still* struggle saying I'm a writer when strangers ask what I do for a living. Until I started making some decent income in freelance writing in 2019, I never made any money at *all* as a writer, so I would often tell strangers I was a teacher, because at least that part of my working life put some income in my bank account every month.

I very much believe you should call yourself a writer, and the more you say it aloud, the more you'll actually feel like a writer. Even in the face of friends and family who think what we do is a dumb hobby that won't lead anywhere.

Some of us are luckier than others.

I've been lucky to surround myself with people who for are supportive of my writing endeavors. My best friends are all writers. My parents have been 100% supportive since I started writing short stories in elementary school, and they've still got my back even as I reach ten years of seriously writing fiction and having no traditionally published novels in the world yet.

My partner has always been the least supportive person in my world when it comes to my fiction writing, but he at least understands my love for it, and he gives me the space to pursue this dream. That's sometimes the best you can hope for when it comes to people who don't quite understand that inherent desire to be creative.

So this is one amazing thing about creative writing workshops and conferences, like I discussed before—you surround yourself with other people who *love writing as much as you do.*

It's almost like speaking an alternate language when I meet up with writer friends. We all *get it.* We all understand the struggle and the fight and the passion and the endurance.

So do your best to surround yourself with people who take your writing seriously.

Sometimes you have no control over this part, especially if, say, you're still living with your parents, and they want you to do anything but write. I know it's hard. I know you might question if they're right, if you should pursue something else that has a better chance at financial stability.

The truth of the matter is this: if you believe in your writing, if you know deep down writing makes you happy, you need to do everything you can to push against that negativity and try to surround yourself with more people who support you.

Creative writing workshops are helpful for this. So are conferences that allow you get outside your comfort zone. Sometimes all it takes is one amazing writer friend to open up your whole world and give yourself the permission to write to your heart's desire.

So find that perfect person. Find *all your people*. Do it however you want.

And no matter what, keep writing.

89. Why You Should Always be Working on the Next Project

If you want to be a writer, you need to do one thing: always be working on your next project.

You can't sit around and revise your one precious manuscript to death. You can't query that manuscript to agents and then sit around, glancing at your phone every ten seconds, taking every rejection to heart.

So much of your writing success depends on your willingness to move on to the next thing, whatever it may be. It doesn't have to be another novel right away. It can be a poem. A short story. A flash fiction story, even!

If all you do next is slowly tool away for a few weeks on a 1,000-word story, that can be enough.

If you're ambitious, sure, you can start the next novel. Before I signed with an agent in 2017, that's what I always did.

And for about six years, this was the permanent state of my writing schedule…

1. Novel A on submission to literary agents. Anywhere from twenty to fifty query letters out at any given time.
2. Novel B in the second or later draft. Slowly working away at the latest revision.
3. Novel C on the first draft. There's nothing that will distract you from waiting to hear news about your book on submission than to be deep into writing the first draft of a different book. And also have another manuscript in a later stage of revision, so that will be ready for querying in the coming six to eight months.

For about six years, I wrote two new manuscripts a year. And I *queried* two manuscripts a year.

I always had novels on submission, always had an e-mail inbox revealing a rejection or two every day.

Doing this one thing as a writer always kept me positive about my work when the rejections continued to pour in.

It gave me a sense of clarity, working on the next thing rather than fixate on the last.

It is pivotal to your writing career that you, at the very least, be working on *some kind* of second writing project while your first one's out to agents or publishers.

Do this one thing, and I promise, you'll stay a little bit saner.

Well, we've gone through all the important elements of the novel writing life! I hope you have a better grasp on what you need to work on, from finding your ideas to publishing your work. I hope you feel like you're ready to take on whatever project you're passionate about.

Now? Let's conclude with a few final pieces meant to inspire you…

<u>FINALLY</u>

90. 3 Things I Learned from Writing My Twentieth Novel

In July 2019 I finished my twentieth novel, *Fear of Water.*

Yes, my twentieth. I still haven't quite wrapped my head around the fact that I have now written twenty novels, and that I did it in *less than ten years*. That's about two books a year, which is crazy!

I wrote it fast. I started writing on June 3 and then finished on July 3. The first draft came in at 81,000 words, a solid word-count for a young adult novel. The last week of the process I was averaging 3,500 words a day, up from 2,200 words a day where I started in early June.

So what did I learn from this process? What's changed since I wrote my *first* novel way back in 2010? What's gotten better, and is there anything that's gotten worse?

Here are *three things* I learned from writing my twentieth novel…

1. The writing doesn't get easier.

This is the big, sad reality of novel writing. At least it is in my case. You'd think after nineteen books I'd be able to finally write a first draft that came easily, that just flowed right off my fingertips from day one. Yes, there were scenes in my latest novel that were lots of fun, and I was happy to slowly but surely figure out the arc of my story and the depth to my characters.

But the writing itself wasn't easier. In fact, in a sense, the writing has become *harder* in the last couple years because I actually feel more pressure now than I did with the early books. When I was writing up a storm in 2010 and 2011, I felt free to make mistakes. I didn't overthink anything. I genuinely enjoyed almost every second of the process.

Now, however, the pressure is on. I've completed an MFA in Creative Writing, and I've been going after this dream for ten years now. In some way I don't feel I have the option to screw up another one. I don't have the option to make more mistakes.

I haven't been traditionally published yet, and after writing twenty novels, there's a tendency to ask myself why. Am I not good enough? Will I never be good enough? Will I never get a book published even I end up writing *another* twenty novels?

I wanted the first draft of my latest to go seamlessly, to feel really, really good every day. And while I feel great about the manuscript now (I recently completed the third draft), and I'm excited to query the book in the months to come, many of the writing days on that first draft were super difficult. Like, where I would stress over a single sentence for twenty minutes. Where I'd write a whole page… then erase it and start over. Where I'd question a character's motivation in chapter six while I was currently working on chapter ten.

All sorts of things went wrong, and worse, I often found myself tearing my hair out in a few tough places in the story. I wanted to scream (and sometimes did). I wanted to cry (and definitely almost did). Partly because the writing process was hard, like it's always hard—in the words of Tom Hanks in *A League of Their Own*, "the hard is what makes it great"—but also because I've written so many books, and I feel like by now the writing part shouldn't *still* be kicking my ass so much.

Thankfully, at the end of the day, I got 90% or so of my original vision of this novel on the page in that first draft, and I'm ecstatic about that. And two revisions later, it's close to 100%. Remember, always, you don't have to get it exactly right in the first draft. That never changes, whether you're working on your first novel or your twentieth.

2. The one thing that does get easier is hitting the words I want to hit every day.

Although writing novels doesn't necessarily get easier year after year, the one thing I do feel gets easier is making your word counts every day while you're writing.

I really struggled with this in the beginning. Back in 2010, when I wrote my first novel, I aimed for 2,000 words a day for eight straight weeks, and so often I failed to reach that number. I would get to 1,600 words and say, okay, that's enough. There were a few days I stopped at 1,000. Rarely did I actually pass 2,000. I remember having the same struggle on my second novel, too.

But that's never an issue these days. I sit down at my writing desk in the morning, and I decide how many words I want to hit, and I *always* reach that number for the day, even if I only have two hours of writing time. Even if my time is limited, I still reach the word count I set for myself.

On my twentieth novel, I started by aiming for 2,200 words a day. I of course allowed myself to go over that number, but I couldn't go a word under. And I never did.

The absolute lowest amount of words I wrote in a day during that 31-day period was 2,200 words. The most? 4,200 words. That was my marathon final day of writing the last chapter, and I can't even remember the last time I wrote 4,200 words in a single non-stop novel writing session. That was a little bit insane, and it took almost five hours, but I was finishing the novel, so I was able to do it.

Throughout the years you pick up on little tricks to reach your word counts. Like listening to the right music. Like picking the time of day when you're at your most creative (for me it's between 10am and 2pm).

Something I do lately that helps a lot is not think of it as reaching 2,200 words in two hours. I look at trying to hit 500 words in thirty minutes. *That's* the goal I aim to achieve from now on.

When I start writing at 10:30am, I do everything in my power to hit 500 words by 11am. If it takes until 11:05am or 11:10am, fine, but it's a really awful writing day if, say, an hour passes, and I still haven't hit 500 words. That's when I know it's gonna be a very long day.

In the last five years, I've been able to hit my daily word count 100% of the time, and that basically comes from lots and lots of practice.

3. It's okay if you need to take a break.

There were a few other things I learned, of course, and that I've tried to pay closer attention to as more years pass. Take more chances in my storytelling, for one. After twenty books, there's simply no time left to *play it safe*.

Therefore, in my twentieth book, I play with a super cool dual POV structure, one told in first person from the male protagonist and one told in first person from the female protagonist's blog entries. I also bring at least three huge surprises in the second half, including an ending I hope will make readers gasp.

I also have had the tendency throughout the years to pay way more attention to the plot of my story rather than the characters, and especially since completing my MFA in Creative Writing, where I took workshop after workshop and studied craft like never before, I've come to the realization that many of my books in the past have failed because the characters weren't unique enough and didn't have strong enough goals and motivations.

It's not enough, for example, to just have things *happening* to your main character. Your main character needs to be actively going after something, and their actions and decisions need to play a key role in the novel. This is something I never thought enough about in my early years writing novels, but it's something that never escapes my mind now.

One other thing I learned in the writing of my twentieth novel? It's okay if I need to take a break from writing new novels. In ten years of almost non-stop writing there was only one extended break I took that lasted about eighteen months.

And you know what? That break was great! I worked slowly on a revision of my latest novel and lived my life a bit more. I went on more adventures. Left the house more. Traveled more. That year and a half I didn't spend writing every second of the day was kind of wonderful, and it doesn't make you any less of a writer to admit that.

Twenty books is a lot. Twenty books in less than ten years is a hell of a lot! I'll always be proud of that. And I can't wait to get to work on more revisions to come.

But one thing I know for sure is this: I am definitely *not* going to write another twenty books in the *next* ten years. Something big I've learned from writing my twentieth novel is that, ultimately, *there's more to life than writing novel after novel.* There's more to see and do with my time, there's more experiences to have and to cherish with so many people I love.

And I'm thankful that realization came to me sooner rather than later.

You don't *always* have to be writing to be a writer. Never forget that.

91. Why You Need to Write Fiction for Joy, not Money

You should never lose the dream of being able to make money as a fiction writer.

It's not unreasonable to hope for, and expect, to make money from your fiction eventually. We're not just doing it for the sake of the joy of writing. At some point you do need to make some money from your fiction, or you might find yourself burn out or worse, stop writing all together.

It's also perfectly acceptable to write other kinds of things to make some income. Freelance writing, for example. Copyediting and editing and things like that. There's a lot of writing we all do to try to make some income, and there's nothing wrong or shameful about that.

We all have our different circumstances, but there's something to be said about actually getting *paid* for the jobs we do.

Write just to write if you want, but I do think after awhile some income here and there is a very good thing!

The thing is you should never fixate on money while you're writing.

When you're actually doing the writing part itself, *that's* when you shouldn't ever focus on making money. If you're writing a novel, and throughout every chapter you're thinking more about the advance you might be able to make from the book one day rather than immersing yourself in the story and your characters' lives, you're in this for the wrong reasons.

First of all, there is no guarantee you'll ever be able to make money from your fiction writing. I've been at it for ten years now, and I've still made very little. Writing fiction is in no way, shape, or form an easy way to make money, take it from me!

Second of all, the irony is that if you fixate on money while you're drafting your novel, that novel probably won't ultimately be good enough *to ever make you any money.* The more you push the financial aspect aside and just focus on the story itself, the better chance in the long run you might be able to sell the book and be paid for it! Funny how that works, huh?

And third, to put it simply, you should absolutely be writing for the joy of writing, not for making money off it.

Sure, there are some genres that sell better than others. If you write a 130,000-word literary novel, that might be a harder sell than a 90,000-word young adult fantasy novel.

If you want to make money from your fiction, be smart about what kinds of stories you write, but at the same time don't write in a genre you hate just because you think that kind of work will make you money.

Writing should be about joy, first and foremost. To sit down at your writing desk every day obsessed with aspects of money is not a good place you want to be in. No matter what your circumstances may be, write because you love to write. Write because you have things to say and stories to tell.

Write your heart out every single day, keep pushing yourself, take chances, try different kinds of stories and genres, and see where the work takes you. If you keep at it long enough, you *will make money* from your writing eventually.

And you will be happy knowing that the money came from the joy of the work, as it should be!

92. Don't Feel Pressured to Write the Next Blockbuster Novel

"So, are you writing the next Harry Potter?"

I don't know about you, but I get asked this question often enough to make me want to weep. It's maddening to tell a person you've just met that you're a young adult novel writer and then get that common response. I truly do hear it *all the time.*

No, I'm not writing the next Harry Potter. And more importantly, I wouldn't even know *how* to write the next Harry Potter.

That series was a case of lightning in a bottle. Something incredible that came around at just the right time and became a phenomenon unlike any other. It simply can't be replicated. Even if I go on to write another fifty novels, I'll never write anything as popular as J.K. Rowling's beloved series.

You might of course be compelled to write something that reaches even five percent of the popularity of Harry Potter. Something that can reach what's known as blockbuster mentality.

And don't be naive to think that people in the publishing industry aren't looking for the next blockbuster, too.

Until Harry Potter, children's books were never looked at as blockbusters. Some books sold better than others, but before Harry Potter, children's books weren't necessarily the go-to for film and TV adaptations, it wasn't the place for massive hits that both kids and adults wanted to read with equal amounts of enthusiasm.

But in the last twenty years or so, kidlit has been looked at as a place for *huge* blockbusters. Nearly every year there's at least one break-out success, and people in the publishing industry are always looking for the next one.

For those of us who write books for children and teenagers, we should at least be *aware* of the blockbuster mentality. And we should be aware that books in children's literature are expected to *make money.*

That second part of course goes to books in most markets. That book you spend months or years on and revised with an agent and then sold to an editor is expected to earn everybody *some* income. You should be writing the book you want to write, but you should also be thinking about your market and your genre expectations.

At the same time though, don't ever feel pressured to write the next blockbuster novel.

That's a place no author ever wants to be in. If you write your next book *expecting* it to be a blockbuster, odds are you'll be disappointed in the end, and worse, your book will probably lack any heart because what was at the forefront of your mind while writing it was money.

Yes, you should want to earn income from your writing, and you should hope to sell your next novel. But to write a novel strictly for money, in the hopes that it might turn into some kind of blockbuster, is an illogical exercise. There are so many other ways to earn a living, after all. There are so many other things you can do.

Hope for the best with your writing career, always, but when it comes to the actual writing of your next novel, write the story that compels you. Tell a story you *want to tell*. If it turns into a blockbuster, then great. If it doesn't? Then that's fine, too.

Whatever you do, don't feel that pressure. Just keep loving the process, tell the best stories you can, and eventually amazing things will happen.

93. Why You Need to Remember the Magic of Writing

It can be difficult to forget the magic part when you're deep into a writing project.

When you're in the weeds of the seventh draft or struggling with the end of a scene halfway through the first draft or re-reading the closing scene for the forty-ninth time.

So much of writing is indeed about tools and carpentry, about words and style. You can't write a book without them.

And the more you understand how to utilize the tools as your disposal, the more you experiment with your words and style, the better your work will be in the long run.

You have to master the basics. You have to fail often. You have to try new styles, new genres, new kinds of characters and stories.

And you have to never, never, forget the magic.

I have tough days when I'm writing. Endless moments of self-doubt.

After I've spent years writing multiple novels, you'd think I sit down at the computer now filled with confidence, knowing exactly how to do this. I have more experience now than I did in my twenties, I've written way more novels than I ever imagined I could.

Yet every time I sit down to write, whether it's new prose or a current revision, there's always a little bit of fear.

That I'll mess up the scene. That I won't get the images in my head down on paper exactly as I'd like.

That the scene actually worked better in the third draft and now in the fifth draft I'm making it worse.

Writing a novel is an extremely difficult and arduous process.

It's not enough to just write a first draft, maybe do a polish or two, and be done with it.

If you're serious about writing, you have to not only commit to completing a first draft but then spend many months or even years to revise it to the point where everything works—the story, the characters, the pacing, the surprises. Sometimes you nail it fast. Sometimes it takes awhile.

And sometimes you step away from the computer feeling less than, feeling like if you had more talent you could make the manuscript work.

No matter what, keep going anyway.

If you work hard on your writing and keep improving, there's the possibility you'll be traditionally published eventually. There's the possibility that readers all around the world might one day get to discover your characters and your narratives you're tried to make unique and compelling.

But what should keep you going the most… is the magic. The pure magic of storytelling. The way, with just words, you can create an entire world and live there for the longest time.

The magic I felt as a kid when I read my first books sometimes gets lost when I'm working hard on the latest draft of my new book.

But when it comes back, when I remember that magic in all its forms, the work stops being work, and the joy of writing comes through in ways I never expect.

Writing is hard. Writing and revising a novel is *really* hard. But as long as you keep the magic alive, there's no telling what you'll be able to achieve.

94. Why Writing Can Heal You Physically and Mentally

What healed Stephen King after Bryan Smith hit him and almost killed him in 1999 with a Dodge van?

Sure, there were lots that helped him during that trying time. His family, of course. And luck as well. King talks in his craft book *On Writing* about how if the truck had struck him just *a few inches* to the left or right, he might have been killed on impact. It's terrifying to read about how close King came close to death on that fateful June day more than twenty years ago.

But one element that helped heal King a great deal? His writing, of course!

Five weeks after he almost died, and before he was even able to finish the first draft of *On Writing*, he sat up and began to write again. Writing in so many ways brought him *back to life*.

There truly is a healing aspect to writing.

I have been lucky enough to not be a situation where I needed writing to heal me physically, to bring me back to life in a way.

But writing certainly healed Stephen King. He talks in *On Writing* how difficult it was to write for long periods of time during his healing process. He could only sit up for so long before the pain hit, and then he'd have to take a break. He ultimately couldn't write as much day after day as he would have wanted to.

But even that small amount of time writing each day absolutely helped heal him bit by bit, both mentally and physically.

When you're in the zone as a writer, I truly believe you leave your body. You become one with the words, and the story takes over. When I really get rolling, everything in my own life takes a back seat to what's happening in my narrative.

And you truly do forget about your problems, both mentally and physically.

Writing helped Stephen King heal in both ways. More than two decades since his accident, he is in good shape physically and he's still writing fantastic books mentally.

Writing took King to a place that another person who didn't write might never have been able to reach.

Write because you love writing. Write for whatever reason you want. But remember it's also a tremendous way to heal.

I love to write for all sorts of reasons. I love writing because I love stories and characters. I love to get lost in narratives that takes me out of my real life. I love the feeling that happens when your characters take over and you find yourself in an out-of-body experience.

But always remember that writing has the ability to heal, both mentally and physically. I've sat down to write on bad days, where I was feeling down or depressed about things, and writing helped.

I've sat down to write on days I didn't feel well, like having a cold or having a terrible stomachache, and yes, writing *helped*.

Writing absolutely has the ability to heal. It played a major role in healing Stephen King, it's healed me throughout the years, and it can heal you, too.

There's simply no reason to not be writing as much as possible. If you love to write, keep writing, and do it every day.

There's no telling how much benefit it will add to your life!

95. 3 Things to be Thankful for as a Writer

So much of the writing life is a constant struggle.

———

You struggle to come up with words to put down on the page. You struggle to come up with new ideas. You struggle to make any money. You struggle to get anybody to believe in the work that you're doing.

You struggle sometimes to believe you have any value as a writer yourself.

I've been writing almost every day for ten years, and I still feel these things all the time.

But what I try to do now more than ever before is be thankful for everything in my life that writing has brought me. Because even though I don't yet have a novel on the shelves yet or have millions of adoring fans awaiting my every word, there's simply *so much* to be thankful for.

Here are *three* of them…

1. The ability to express yourself in ways few people ever can.

I genuinely don't understand how people get through their days, weeks, months, without at least occasionally writing their thoughts down on paper.

It doesn't have to be published. Nobody has to ever read it.

But the millions of people out there who never write a word down and keep their thoughts completely internal for all their lives… how do they do it? How do they not go insane?

Writing is the outlet for me that allows my life to have balance, that allows me to vent my frustrations and ideas and dreams down on paper. Whether it's thoughts about my own life or in the lives of imagined characters.

Any kind of writing helps you express yourself, whether it's fiction or non-fiction. It's therapeutic. It enriches the soul.

And it saddens me that many people out there don't feel the need or desire to do that. Every single person who ever lived has at least one great story to tell. Every person could enrapture a reader for dozens of pages, if not hundreds. But people prefer to keep it bottled up inside or simply vent to a family member, friend, or partner.

Being a writer means you get to express yourself in a variety of ways that ultimately leads to a life well lived. And how can we not be thankful for that?

2. The ability to escape your own reality and enter the world of others.

Life can get hard at times. And writing down your thoughts on paper *isn't always enough*.

Sometimes you need to get away from yourself sometimes. Get away from your circumstances, your reality. You want to escape through any means possible.

Non-writers escape their realities in a variety of ways, like reading or watching movies or scrolling mindlessly through their phones. There are all sorts of ways.

But writers get to take things one step further by completely entering the worlds of other people. By surrendering to a world of fiction that often feels just as real, if not more so, than the life you're living right now.

There is this magical place you go to as a writer when you're zipping along in the newest scene you're writing, the newest chapter. It's the zone. It's a place that is happy and amazing. A place that allows you to step outside yourself and stay put in the world of your imagination.

Writers get to do this *as much as they want*. I had it numerous times this past summer writing my latest novel. I had it this past September when I wrote a new short story.

Most people don't get to escape their own realities in ways that are healthy and good. Writers get to do it every day if they want, how cool is that?

3. The ability to make a difference in people's lives.

This is, of course, the big one. One of the main reasons I do what I do.

I mean, let's be honest about something. Most of us would still write even if we knew nobody was ever going to read anything we wrote, and that definitely includes me. So much of what I've written in my life honestly *hasn't* been read by very many people, and I'm okay with that.

I've had the writing bug since I was a kid, and nothing has ever stopped me from writing, even when it was in journals, even when it was just freewriting.

But the ability to make a difference in people's lives? Now *that's* something that means a lot to writers.

Because so often we're writing for ourselves, and we don't realize how powerful words can be, that there are readers out there we will never meet who will be moved and touched and changed by the stories we tell.

Whether those stories are fiction or non-fiction. Whether those stories were written for a specific audience or just for yourself.

I know there might be times when you think nothing you write matters, that nobody will ever pay any attention to your stories, that you won't ever make a difference in a single person's life.

The truth is you will. You can. You already *have*.

Because you're a writer. And always will be.

96. Why You Should Embrace Failure as a Writer

The beginning of your writing career will be filled with lots and lots of failure.

I sometimes think about all the hardship I've had over the past ten years to get where I am as a writer today. Twenty novels. Dozens of short stories. An MA degree in English and an MFA degree in Creative Writing.

And thousands upon thousands of rejection slips.

I wonder that if I could go back to my 2009 self who was thinking of abandoning the dream of film-making for novel writing and told him what I have been through to get to this point, I'm not so sure I would have ever tried the writing life.

It's lonely. There's little stability. There's not any guarantee for success.

And what is success, anyway?

Is success having a novel traditionally published? Right now, that's how I think of success, but having just one book traditionally published doesn't in any way mean I'm going to be a successful author.

It's a great next step, one I really hope is in my near future, but that's what it is really: the next step.

And that's why you have to love writing. You have to get up every day wanting to spend a few hours in another world. You want to spend more time with your characters. You want to put your thoughts down on paper.

If all you think about is the monetary outcome, you're never going to make it as a writer.

Times will be tough at the beginning. You might be one of the lucky ones and find success quickly, within the first couple years. Your first book might be the one that lands you an agent and a publishing deal.

Or maybe it's your second or third. Or even your fifteenth.

There's no guarantee that anything is going to come of this no matter how hard you work at it. There's just not, and that's the sad truth.

However, as long as you keep writing, the possibility of success will continue to grow.

I haven't found success yet, but I hope it's out there for me, somewhere in the future. Maybe in the next year or two. Hopefully *this* year.

In the meantime, all that's left to do is keep writing, keep trying.

And keep believing.

One day, maybe when you're least expecting it, and maybe when you need it most, success will find its way to you.

And all that failure you endured… will have been worth it.

97. Writing is a Difficult and Lonely Life. Do It Anyway.

Writing isn't something you should go into lightly.

The writing life is often extremely lonely. You're by yourself most of the day, and you don't really talk to anybody. When you do leave the house and go see your friends and family, the talking part noticeably comes with a bit more difficulty.

Because you've been so immersed in your amazing story and your fascinating characters that real life actually feels like fiction sometimes, not the other way around.

It's often hard when you're in the midst of a new writing project to give real life your all. Even though when you're by yourself all day you feel like you should be spending more time with other people. And then of course when you're with those people, you want to go right back into the isolation of your writing room. Oh, the irony.

Yes, writing is lonely. Writing is difficult. Writing might not be the ideal life. It might not be the healthiest life.

But you know what? Do it anyway.

You're going to struggle coming up with new ideas. Have trouble figuring out a basic outline to your latest story. Think for weeks and weeks about your characters and what makes them unique, what makes them tick.

Do it anyway.

You're going to struggle in your writing from day one. You might stare at a blank page for an hour or longer, trying a bunch of new first sentences which you then quickly delete. You'll enter week two, week three, in a state of despair because the writing of your new novel isn't matching what you envisioned in your head. It's 10%, 20%, of the book you wanted to write.

Do it anyway.

You're going to have days when you want to quit. Days when the words just aren't coming. You'll be halfway through the novel but want to abandon it and move onto something else. You'll feel at times that you totally suck and that you have no business writing. You'll want to pull your hair out and pound your fist against the wall and scream at the top of your lungs.

Trust me, I'm telling you—keep writing anyway.

Because every writer feels like this.

Every writer has moments of self-doubt in the drafting process, in the revising process. In the before, during, and after of writing.

To have no doubt at all and think you're the greatest writer in history is not a place you want to be. That kind of thinking will get you nowhere.

You should doubt yourself to some extent. You should question certain choices you've made. You should occasionally leave your writing desk feeling frustrated, even angry.

It happens to all of us. It's just a part of the process. What's most important is that you *keep going*. Keep writing. Finish things. Revise your latest novel over and over and make it the best it can be.

If the idea of sitting in dark rooms for years on end creating new stories and characters doesn't interest you, then by all means, do something else. If the idea of writing compels you, though, you need to give yourself over to it, and remember always that it's going to be difficult, it's going to be lonely.

But at the same time, it's so very worth it. The writer's life is a great life, never forget that.

Because no matter how difficult and lonely it gets, *you're creating stories.* You're making art. You're opening up whole new worlds to other readers through your creative imagination.

And there's nothing more fulfilling that.

98. Why You Need to Stop Calling Yourself an Aspiring Writer

You want to hear a sad, dirty secret?

On many days I still consider myself *an aspiring writer.*

Even though I've been writing pretty much every day for ten years, I *still* after all this time sometimes consider myself an aspiring writer. Why?

Because I don't have a novel traditionally published yet.

And since that's been the number one goal from day one, since April 2010 when I decided I wanted to be a published novelist, part of me still feels like I'm aspiring because *that hasn't happened yet.*

Sure, I've gotten close. I signed with a literary agent in 2017, we worked on my middle grade horror novel *Monster Movie* for a year, and then it went out to editors at major publishing houses for a year and a half. A lot of editors really liked it. We got close with a couple of them.

But it didn't happen. And I'm starting the querying process over again with a new manuscript I believe in with my whole heart.

So today? After all that time and effort I've put into writing in the past decade? Part of me continues to feel like an aspiring writer. Someone who's done a lot of great work but is not fully accomplished yet, since my main goal hasn't been met.

But you know what? We all need to nix that damn word from our vocabulary once and for all.

Calling ourselves aspiring writers is the same way of thinking as telling people what our real jobs are when they ask what we do. Since I've been teaching for seven years, I often will tell people I'm a teacher, not a writer. The writing aspect of my life won't even come up.

Again, why? Because teaching helps pays the bills more than writing does.

It's something that needs to stop, for me, and for you. If writing is your passion, if it's your jam, tell people you're a writer when they ask you what you do. And if they ask a follow-up about how you make money doing that, or make a snide comment suggesting what you do is worthless, ignore that person and move along.

Tell people you're a writer, and not an aspiring writer. Toss that terrible word in the trash, I'm telling you.

The definition of aspiring is simply this: *directing one's hopes or ambitions toward becoming a specified type of person.*

You know why the word is stupid, especially in this case? Because you're already that type of person. You're already a writer if you're doing the actual writing.

Sure, you can have hopes and ambitions for your writing career. You can have *big* hopes and ambitions that haven't been met yet. They haven't been met for me after ten years of hard work, and I'm OK with that.

But just because you haven't reached the ultimate dream doesn't mean you or I should call ourselves aspiring writers.

Drop that dumb word, I mean it. Call yourself a writer. Because you already are.

The writing life is hard enough without thinking of yourself as *less than*. As a person who's working toward something always and not as a person who's already accomplished and special, which you are.

It takes guts just to write at all. It takes confidence and resilience to sit in front of a computer every day and pour your heart out on the page.

So many people *talk* about writing. About what they want to write in the future. About the novel that's in their heart.

That's not writing. That's not even aspirational writing. That's just conversation.

If you're actually putting your butt in the chair every day and writing? Whether or not it makes you money?

Then you're a writer. You're not an aspiring writer. You're doing the work. You're learning. You're getting better. You're honing your skills. You're improving your craft. You're having fun. You're doing well. And you're going places, I'm telling you.

You're a writer.

99. Why You Should Dream of Success as a Writer, and Dream Big

Deep down, I know I'm not going to make four hundred thousand dollars from my fiction writing anytime soon. I know I'll probably never make anything close.

And yet it's fun to think about it, isn't it?

When you've worked extremely hard every day for *years* on your writing, isn't it amusing to think about maybe, one day, striking gold?

Whether it be your first book that sells (unlikely) or your seventh book that sells (more likely).

It's a tricky dilemma because you don't want to write fiction if making money is your number one goal.

If you sit down at your laptop every day to write the new chapter of your novel thinking about how many copies the book might sell or how many hundred-dollar-bills will come dumping out of the sky onto your head when the manuscript sells.

Your job is to tell a great story and create amazing characters your readers want to go on a journey with. You can't think about monetary success when you're writing fiction.

At the same time, you are absolutely allowed to dream.

Try not to dream about success while you're actually in the middle of writing your words and pages for the day. Your focus should be on the writing itself.

But later in the day, when you're jogging or walking the dog or waking up from a nap, go ahead and dream about what could happen in the future.

And let the dream be whatever you want it to be.

For instance, I don't really dream about riches when it comes to my fiction writing career. I don't sit around and hope that maybe I'll have a book sell for an astronomical amount of money (although, of course, I wouldn't mind such a predicament either!).

Honestly, what I dream about the *most* is having thousands of readers for my fiction, particularly children. *So* many children reading my middle grade and young adult novels and sending me letters and reaching out to me online and begging me for the next book, whatever it may be.

Being at a place where readers are talking about my work and sharing it with friends is the dream for me. Whether or not that translates to huge monetary success. Whether or not someone calls me on the phone and tells me my book just sold for four hundred thousand dollars.

Tons of readers will always be my dream. Find the dream that works for you.

Making money to sustain my way of life is a dream too, of course, and so is publishing multiple books over many years and decades.

In the end, whatever the dream may be for you, allow yourself to think it, believe it, hope for it.

Dreams are good for the soul, and they are necessary for writers because dreams keep us going.

So keep writing, keep believing.

———

And dream big always.

100. Start Writing Your Novel Today, not Tomorrow!

Here's the thing: if you want to write a novel this year, you should start writing it this month.

Not next month, not next year. In fact you should start writing it today, not tomorrow!

There's always going to be a long list of excuses. You don't have the time (the big reason). You're afraid of screwing up (the second big reason). You haven't done an outline. You don't know the first scene. You don't know your ending. The characters aren't fully developed yet.

There's *always* going to be an excuse. Even if you have nothing to do for the next six weeks. Even if you have no responsibilities at all. (Wouldn't that be nice, right?)

Because the truth is that novel writing is hard. I still struggle every day I sit down to write, I do! There was one particular novel I kept putting off for the longest time. I couldn't figure out the point-of-view, I couldn't figure out my main character. So I kept pushing it back year after year until finally last summer I decided it was time to write it.

I messed up the first draft at times, just like I always do. Some of the chapters were too long, and the ending was rushed, and the main conflict wasn't always compelling enough.

But what's one really great thing I did last summer? *I wrote the novel.* After two years of thinking about that story, I finally put it down on paper. And by now I've finished the third draft, and the novel is coming together in a way I'm super happy with. Hooray!

Never forget it all starts with the first draft. Nothing can ever happen with a bunch of blank paper. You've got to get the story down first as best you can.

And you know what's fairly easy to do during the novel drafting process once you put your mind to it?

Finding time every day to reach a desired word count, and then sticking to that schedule every day until you reach the end.

Like I've been saying this entire book, the easiest way to finish your novel is to decide on a word count and then stick to that word count until you reach the final word of your manuscript.

I decided in May 2019 I was going to write 2,200 words a day on my latest novel seven days a week. That would get to me 15,400 words by the end of week one, and that would get me to 77,000 words by the end of week five.

Five weeks to write a novel. Seems crazy, right? But, again, if you put your mind to it, you can get it done. You can absolutely do this!

Sure, you can write your book with just 200 words a day or just 500 words a day, too. And it's true. You can. If you want to go the slow route, by all means, go for it.

The important thing is that you write it now, not later. I thought about writing my latest novel in the fall. Or waiting until winter break. I wasn't sure if I was ready to write this one. I wasn't sure if I had the talent, or the energy, or the willingness to carry it through.

But I pushed past my fears, my reservations, and I did it. And by July 2019 I had a completed first draft of the book.

So if you've been thinking about writing a novel this year, stop thinking about it, and do it!

Start today, not tomorrow. Give yourself permission to screw up. Give yourself permission to not meet your writing schedule on a day here and there.

It's okay if you write five days a week instead of seven. It's okay if lots of mistakes are made.

The point is to finish your first draft however you can. Finish the first draft, and then the real work begins. Finish the first draft… and then you're well on your way to becoming a successful novel writer.

So please—give yourself permission, finally, to *write your novel.*

Not next year. Not next month. Not tomorrow.

Today.

CONCLUSION

I've learned a hell of a lot about novel writing since I wrote my first book way back in 2010. And there's still more to learn in 2020 and beyond, that much is for sure.

But what's most important of all is to keep trying every day, keep taking chances, keep improving in your writing and the way you go about drafting, revising, editing, and publishing your work.

Like with most everything in life, you need to commit to your writing to be successful. You can't just talk about it with friends. You need to do it! Novel writing might seem scary at first, but I promise if you put in the hard work and energy, you'll find your groove eventually.

Hopefully these 100 tips and strategies I've presented to you in this book will help you write your amazing novel in the weeks and months to come.

I wish you only the best!

ABOUT THE AUTHOR

Brian Rowe received his MFA in Creative Writing and MA in English-Writing from the University of Nevada, Reno. He's written twenty novels, dozens of short stories, five feature-length screenplays, and hundreds of essays.

CONNECT WITH BRIAN ONLINE

Brian's Web Site
http://brianrowebooks.com

Brian's Facebook Author Page
http://facebook.com/brianroweauthor

Brian's Twitter
http://twitter.com/mrbrianrowe